Messages From Mother....
Earth Mother

Also by Mare Cromwell

If I gave you God's phone number....
Searching for Spirituality in America

MESSAGES FROM MOTHER....
EARTH MOTHER

MARE CROMWELL

PAMOON
PRESS

Pamoon Press
Frederick, Maryland
www.pamoonpress.com

Published by Pamoon Press,
an imprint of Sacred Dog Productions LLC.

ISBN 978-0-9717032-3-0

Library of Congress Control Number: 2012916986

Book design by Robert Shelley/www.shelleyllc.com
Cover illustration by Larry Moore/Illustration Source
Author photograph by Andrea Prendki McCluskey

Pamoon Press
Frederick, Maryland
www.pamoonpress.com

www.messagesfrommother.org

Printed in the United States of America.

1 3 5 7 9 10 8 6 4 2

First Edition

For the Future Generations of All Species

CONTENTS

AUTHOR'S NOTE

Where this information comes from is part of the Great Mystery to me. This book was written in only five weeks. I was focused on a completely different book and Spirit broadsided me in late June, 2012, and told me this was the book that I was meant to write. I was fighting lymphoma and essentially surrendered to Spirit to write this. I healed from the cancer during the same time period.

At times Spirit will just do that.

As I understand it, for most of our human existence many peoples across the planet could listen to Spirit. The plants told them about their medicinal properties. The stones shared their stories of ancient, ancient times and stored memories. The trees spoke of a wisdom that only trees, or standing ones, as the Native peoples say, could know.

When someone learns to listen then Spirit will begin to talk and you can sometimes tune in. When Spirit starts to communicate with you, it is a humbling experience and you realize that two-leggeds have only a tiny slice of the greater reality of Life.

You could say I've learned how to listen to some degree.

I've spent the better part of sixteen years studying with Native American teachers and listening to the land. For fifteen of those years, I had a professional gardening business based on an approach I call Sacred Gardening. We tried to do everything from a place of reverence.

My background is also in environmental work. I was a National Park Service Ranger in the Grand Canyon and Alaska in my early twenties and eventually received my Masters in natural resources, which led into international work in the 1990s. That evolved into leading workshops about environmental sustainability on the corporate level on a part-time basis.

It is truly from the outdoor space of hiking or gardening plus learning more of a Native American worldview that allowed my listening to develop. It's tough to learn how to listen in an office setting.

I am not unique. There are so many people waking up and learning how to tune in to the wisdom of the plants, trees and stones. These are hopeful signs in these interesting times.

My first book is called *If I gave you God's phone number....Searching for Spirituality in America*. So it's easy to conclude that I'm open to the concept of communicating with the spiritual realms, the realms of the mystics.

I believe Spirit has messages for us all if we learn to honor this wisdom from our spiritual guides, and just stop to listen. Sometimes it might even be Earth Mother communicating. Surrendering to their wisdom is one of the wisest paths to take.

Meeting Mother

in the Forest

It was a beautiful clear Saturday in April. Sarah, an attractive red-haired woman in her early thirties, was out for a long hike at a large mountain park in Virginia that day. She was feeling rather distraught. Her boyfriend Daniel had told her the night before that he wanted his freedom to take off and travel the country. Her life felt dismal and she needed to be in the woods.

Sarah's heart was aching from Daniel's surprise announcement. On top of that, she'd been barely able to handle watching the news for the past few months. All the killings, fighting in the Middle East, droughts and floods—it was all so overwhelming. The familiar tentacles of depression were starting to take hold.

She hoped that a brisk hike on one of the longer mountain trails in the park would help boost her mood. Being out in nature always helped Sarah feel more balanced and happier. There was something about the ambiance of wild spaces that healed her.

On this particular early spring day, the forest was still and there were no other hikers. Just being out in the fresh mountain air and moving her muscles was helping to shift Sarah's perspectives about her life. Daniel had been feeling restless for months. She did want him to be happy. If he felt called to hit the road and be an adventurer, she wanted to give him her full blessings. Maybe it would be a good thing for her to be single for a while, too. The hiking gave her space to muse, yet her heart still hurt.

Sarah loved hiking. She started to daydream about how fantastic it would be if someone hired her to hike. What bliss that would be. She loved being a pre-school teacher but she'd rather be outside in the mountains all day. Oh, the mountains she could climb, the great leg muscles she'd develop. Her mind strayed from noticing the trees and bushes along the trail to pondering the jobs she could find that would issue biweekly checks for hiking all the trails she'd ever want to hike. Maybe she could even get paid for articles about her hikes. She loved to write, too.

As Sarah was daydreaming, she came around a bend in the trail and suddenly stopped. To her shock, a roundish older woman who looked like someone from the Middle Ages stood in front of her. The woman was average height and dressed in long, rather dirty dark layers of skirts made of a heavy, coarse material Sarah had never seen before. Her gray hair was pulled back from her beautifully weathered wide face, and a full buxom chest filled out the whitish, splotched peasant shirt she wore. Sarah guessed that this strange person must be in her mid-fifties. She stared at the woman.

The woman gazed back at Sarah with the most gentle and compassionate eyes Sarah had ever seen. This woman felt so ... so familiar, Sarah thought to herself, though she knew she had never met her before. Yet there was such a warm feeling to her. Instantaneously Sarah felt at ease around her, which was highly unusual since Sarah generally felt very nervous around strangers.

"Well, aren't you even going to say hello?" The woman finally said in a deep husky tone with a strange sounding accent Sarah could not quite make out.

Her voice startled Sarah. "Oh! Sorry ... So rude of me! I ... well ...

I really did not know what to say to you. You ... well, you seem so different, as if you're not from this world and maybe I was dreaming and you really don't exist. I have been really stressed out and ..."

"Oh, I exist, all right. I definitely exist. Yep. In more ways than you realize," the woman interrupted Sarah.

"Who are you?" Sarah blurted out. Then it struck her that her blunt question was a very insensitive way to speak to an elder.

"Oh, honey, well ... who I am is a long story. A very long story. But I'll give you the short version. This may seem rather a shock to you, but I'm the *Mother* of this planet. I'm Earth Mother. Some call me Gaia. Some call me just plain Mother. In the Andes, many two-leggeds call me Pachamama. I have different names from culture to culture and language to language."

As she was talking, Mother watched Sarah's jaw drop lower and lower.

"Yes, I know it is hard for you to believe that I'm Earth Mother and that I'm talking with you. This is not an everyday occurrence. I know this. You can come over here and pinch me if you want. I am real," she added.

"Ah, that's okay ..." Sarah said, shaking her head. How can a person just go up and pinch Earth Mother—if this really was Earth Mother? This was all too weird. Part of Sarah wanted to turn around and run. This was stretching her comfort zone beyond anything she had ever experienced before. Yet she was amazed at how safe and at ease she felt around this woman, this so-called Earth Mother in the funny-looking clothing. She could not turn and run. She was transfixed by this woman's presence.

Sarah reached her right hand down to her thigh and pinched it through her pants to ensure she was not dreaming. She definitely felt the pain. This really was happening.

"Honey, I know this is way out of the ordinary. Believe me, I know this. It is extremely rare for me to appear to a two-legged. But I've been waiting for you. I know your boyfriend broke up with you last night. Yes, I know his name is Daniel and you really care about him. And your heart hurts so much right now. I know you've been fighting off depression and you'd rather be paid to hike mountain trails more than anything else," Mother said.

Dumbfounded, Sarah wondered how this woman knew all of this about her. Maybe this actually was Earth Mother? Still, nothing from her childhood Presbyterian church had taught her anything about meeting an older woman on a trail who claimed to be *The Mother* of the whole planet.

On the other hand, she had been reading more about Native American spirituality in the past few years. *Black Elk Speaks, The Wind is My Mother* and some of Hyemeyohsts Storm's and Jamie Sams' books were doggy-eared and piled by her bed at her apartment this very day. She had started to embrace the concept of an Earth Mother who was the planet's consciousness. But one that showed up on the trail as an older woman dressed in funny-looking clothes was stretching it!

Mother continued, "You have a beautiful heart, and I know how much you care about the environment and how much sorrow you experience with all the hard news that your culture broadcasts about what is going on around the world. Your papers and televisions don't cover most of the worst of it. Fukushima. The US Navy testing terribly painful sonar waves in the ocean that are killing dolphins and injuring whales. The toxins spewing into the ground and groundwater, and on and on. I know how you have been feeling so overwhelmed by all of this. Believe me, I'm not happy about any of it either."

Sarah looked at the ground and nodded sadly. What this woman was sharing was all true.

"Sarah, I know this is a stretch for you to believe that you are talking with me, Earth Mother. But I need your help. I've been watching you for a while, and I know you are the two-legged who can do this. I know you've been signing the environmental petitions and going to the marches and doing other things, like many of the others who love me. I know you've been feeling such love for me. You can help me directly. You can get my message out to the world, share my thoughts about all of these things and more. I need a two-legged to do it, and you're a good writer and I like you a lot." Mother gave Sarah a warm smile as she said these things.

Sarah listened to Mother's request and realized that part of her great sadness and depression was because she did feel so powerless with all of the terrible environmental trends. She'd been filling out every petition that came into her email inbox and giving small checks to some environmental and socially progressive groups, but didn't feel she was making much of a difference. Maybe she could truly help in other ways. Maybe this really was Earth Mother. This woman was not any ordinary woman—that was certain. For one, she was psychic. Plus, her clothes were too different. And, there was that weird accent she had. But what was most convincing was that Mother oozed love. A warm, cozy love that felt so kind and compassionate. The aroma of roses wafted around her, even though there were no rose bushes anywhere around on that trail. Sarah just noticed that, too. All of a sudden Sarah had an overwhelming desire to go up and be hugged by Mother.

"Honey, you can hug me if you want," Mother said.

Sarah dropped her daypack and stumbled forward into Mother's arms. Mother took her in and held her close. Sarah gradually let herself relax into Mother's chest and felt her heart begin to release what felt like a cloudburst of pain and sorrow. The tears swelled and before she knew it, she was sobbing into Mother's chest and Mother was caressing her head gently.

"That's okay, honey, you just go ahead and cry. Just let it out. I know your heart has been carrying so much. Your beautiful heart ..." Mother said.

Sarah had no idea she harbored so much sadness and sorrow. She cried and cried and cried as Mother held her, until finally there were no more tears to come out, just a few heaving sighs. Mother loosened her arms but held onto Sarah's hands as Sarah stepped back from her. Mother looked her in the eyes and said softly, "I love you so much. You are one of my daughters."

Mother put her right hand on the heart space between Sarah's breasts and held it there for a few moments. As she did this Sarah felt a gentle warmth come into her chest, move into her torso from where Mother's hand was resting, and then out to her arms and legs.

Mother smiled and removed her hand and stepped back from Sarah.

Sarah stood there for several moments feeling a little woozy. The energy Mother had given her seemed to wash her spirit body gently as it moved through her physical body. She felt lighter and more positive than she could ever remember.

"Whoa. Thank you. That was intense ... I had no idea I had that much sorrow in me. It feels as if you ... this is hard to put into words. You ... healed my heart," Sarah said.

"Yes, honey, I did. I can heal all sorts of things. My work really is to heal. There is so much healing needed these days. So much ..." Mother sighed.

"You really are Earth Mother," Sarah said.

"Yes, sweetie, I really am," Mother gave Sarah a deep smile that was so beautiful, it sent another energy wave through Sarah that made her feel more joyful than she'd ever been in her life. It was as if she were glowing.

"Wow. You're amazing," Sarah said.

"Honey, I'm just Earth Mother. A rather tired Earth Mother, for that matter."

"Yeah, I bet that's true." Sarah paused for a few moments. How could she say no to this invitation from Earth Mother? This really must be her. It would be beyond words to work with her. She wanted to pinch herself again to be certain she wasn't dreaming. But it was *real*. This was definitely happening.

"Okay," Sarah finally said. "I'd like to help. I'd love to help. As a matter of fact, I'm not sure if I want to go back to my lonely apartment and my job at all. Can't I just stay here with you?"

Mother shook her head and said, "Oh, honey, I'm afraid that won't work. You have your life to live in your two-legged world. And I need you to be in that world to share my messages. I am only here in front of you right now, looking like an older woman, so you and I can meet today. We can certainly meet again and again, which I hope we will. And I'll be in this human body all those times in the future for our meetings. But most of the time I'm not in a human body. I'm the wind, the birds, the trees, the rivers, the volcanoes, the ocean ... ah, yes, the ocean. I can be found in all of those parts of the Earth and more. That's just how I am."

Earth Mother hugged Sarah one more time. "But you and I can meet often where we'll sit down, even have some tea, and I'll give you some messages I'd really love you to share with the rest of the world. I would really love to be able to do that with you. And you can have more hugs. I might even tell some bad jokes too. You wouldn't believe some of the ones I hear. I hope you don't mind bad jokes," Mother laughed.

"Okay," said Sarah, smiling. "I'm definitely up for it. But how am I going to do all of that? How will I get your messages out to the world? I've never published anything, not even a small poem."

"Oh, good! I was so hoping that you'd say Yes! Don't worry about the details right now though. I'll guide you. Now, I'd like to show you where we'll meet. It's a sacred grove near here. Come on, I'll take you," Mother said.

Mother turned around and tromped off into some thick trees beyond the trail. She was remarkably limber and fast, considering her heavy skirts and round body. Sarah practically had to run to keep up with her. They bushwhacked about a quarter of a mile into the woods, and Sarah was spent and pulling branches out of her hair by the time they got to the edge of a beautiful open glade surrounded by oak trees.

As soon as Sarah saw the glade, she completely forgot the branches in her hair and raw scratches on her arms where she'd been thwacked by the underbrush. Its magnificence took her breath away. Along with some thin grasses, there were wildflowers she had never seen before, and she had been a student of the area's wildflowers since her teens. The glade was a perfect oval about sixty feet across and forty feet wide. The towering oaks around it kept it shaded even in the center where there was a hand-hewn wooden chair and small bench with a low table between them.

"Yes, this is quite lovely, isn't it?" said Mother.

Sarah nodded her head as she soaked up the beauty of the grove. Mother then led her into the center and said, "This is where we'll meet. We'll have the most delightful time together. I'm so looking forward to this. Oh, and don't worry, the chairs are quite comfortable to sit in," Mother winked.

Sarah nodded as she continued to absorb the intimate beauty of the glade. It had a quality to it she had never experienced before, a serene vibrancy of joy, it seemed.

There were so many different types of birds flitting around in the branches of the oaks, singing so joyfully. There were some bird species new to Sarah there also. It was all so remarkable and magical.

Mother interrupted her gazing around the glade. "Sarah, I'd love to meet weekly so we can sit down and have some good long visits. There is so much I want to share in these messages."

"Yes, I think I can do that," Sarah responded. She knew she'd rearrange anything in her life to have these meetings with Mother, and quietly prayed no funerals or any other emergency would arise.

"Don't worry, it will all work out for you to make our discussions here," Mother said. "One more thing, I'm going to give you this stone to help you know this did really happen and we shall meet again. I know it may be hard for you to believe we've just met after we part this afternoon." As she was saying this she reached down into the folds of her outer skirt and pulled out a beautiful blue stone that almost matched Sarah's eyes.

"Gosh, that's really stunning," Sarah said as she took the stone and looked at it more carefully.

"Okay, now put that in your pocket and off you go. I've got things I need to tend to elsewhere. Do you see that little gray squirrel at your feet? He'll guide you back to the trail so you can get on home," Mother said in a hurried tone.

Sarah put the stone in her pants pocket and looked down to see a squirrel she hadn't noticed before with a distinct white tuft at the end of his tail. The squirrel caught her glance and immediately started bounding off to the edge of the grove where they had entered.

"But wait! Mother! How will I know what time? And suppose the weather is bad?" Sarah asked anxiously, watching the squirrel take off.

"Don't worry, Sarah, watch the stone. It will turn a different shade of blue in your apartment when I'm calling you to meet. It will be midday. And no fears about the weather. It will all work out. Oh, and this grove exists only for you and me. No one else can find this sacred space. So you won't be able to bring anyone here if you wanted to. One more thing, Mr. Tufts will greet you at the trail to guide you in every time we meet. Now run along. Mr. Tufts is waiting."

With that, Mother turned and briskly walked to the other side of the glade and vanished.

Again, Sarah had to run through the thick trees dodging branches, this time to keep up with Mr. Tufts. He led her back to the trail and then turned around and gave Sarah a quick piercing look that took Sarah aback. She had no idea that squirrels could be that intense. Then Mr. Tufts quickly disappeared into the thick brush in another direction.

Sarah sat down on a log about ten feet down the trail toward the direction of her car and pulled her water bottle out of her daypack. After taking a long swig, she pulled out her cell phone and was stunned to see that only five minutes had passed since the last time she looked at it, just before meeting Mother. How could that be? She began to ponder all the things that had just happened to her that seemed beyond any logic or answer.

She pulled out the blue stone from her pocket and studied it. It was a deep blue with tiny striations of gray in it. She had never seen anything like it and suspected that no scientist had either. The stone was warm from being in her pocket and had a heavy solidness to it. She held it to her heart and felt a faint ripple of Mother's energy again. As she put the stone back in her pocket, she made the commitment to carry it with her everywhere she went. It would be like having Mother's love with her at all times.

After some water and nuts, Sarah decided to head back down the trail to go home. She did not feel the need to hike anymore. Her mind was swimming with the day's events. Was it really just five minutes? Had she just experienced a time warp? Her fingers kept being drawn to play with the blue stone in her pocket as she forced herself to accept that the meeting on the trail did just happen. She had met Earth Mother and was going to be seeing her again, often.

Mother said that she'd know when to come back next Saturday just by watching the stone. Sarah wondered what color it would turn and how it would be able to change colors. And how did Mother have the ability to take on a human body like that? The questions bounced around in her head as her sneakers pounded the down-hill trail.

In spite of the slew of questions in her brain, Sarah felt more at peace and happier than she ever remembered. She also knew she could never tell anyone about what happened that afternoon. They'd think she'd gone bonkers.

Whatever she wrote up to publish was all going to be labeled *fiction*. Of this she was certain.

Message 1

Please Love Your Mother.

That's Me,

Earth Mother

Mother: Sarah, it's so great to see you back here again. I see Mr. Tufts brought you in off the trail all safe and sound. You have some branches in your hair. But no worries. They look good on you.

Sarah: Thanks, Mother. Yeah, Mr. Tufts can really fly through all that underbrush, considering how tiny his legs are. I was so excited to see him there on the trail waiting for me just now. Plus, the stone turned the most stunning shade of blue-green earlier, back at my apartment. Almost an ocean teal shade with dark blue around the edges. I was watching it all morning to see if or when it would turn and it did! I'm so excited to be here!

Mother: Yes, yes, I promised you that it would. Good, good. Well, I brought us some tea and some ugli fruit cookies.

Sarah: Ugli fruit?

Mother: Yes, they are kind of like an orange, but uglier. And don't ask me if I made the cookies. I have my ways, you know! The next thing you'll be asking me is whether I have a kitchen I cook in. I can't give away all of my secrets. Can't do that.

As they were talking, Mother pulled out a basket at the base of her bench and proceeded to unpack a beautiful English tea set of bone china along with a matching plate of cookies with a dusted maple sugar coating. She poured each of them a cup of tea and served the cookies. Then she passed out beautifully embroidered pressed napkins. Sarah watched in amazement.

Mother: So, let's get started. The first message I'd like you to transcribe:

Please, learn to love your Mother. Me, your Earth Mother. I give you all a planet full of love. That's what all this evolution is, love in action. All these trees and the food you eat and the air you breathe, it's earthy-love in action. I give all of this to you and love you all so much.

But it is not until you give your love back to me that our relationship can grow. I don't just mean putting a bumper sticker about loving me on your boxes on wheels. I like those and all that. But I mean really love me. Really feel your love for me. I would like a relationship with each and every one of you. I would.

How do you give your love back to me? One of the best ways is to offer blessings to me. You can offer tobacco at the base of a tree that calls to you. Anywhere. Tobacco has such magical properties. I love tobacco. The good tobacco, hopefully grown organically—you know, without all that toxic stuff that I did not create. Or pour some honey on the ground. Or milk. Any kind of offering. You can do this while saying prayers to me. Thanking me. Or the trees. Even the mosquitoes out there biting you. You can thank them too. Just kidding. I know you two-leggeds don't like the mosquitoes so much. Oh, well. So it goes.

Native peoples put out 'spirit plates' full of food when they have big feasts. This shows their love for me, their giving back. Just an example.

Another way is to burn a little smudge in the morning. Oh, you probably don't know what smudge is. Well, there are certain herbs that my beautiful two-leggeds who remember the old ways burn. You can just burn ceremonial white sage, or add cedar to it and other herbs too. This is a wonderful way to send prayers and bless your home or apartment. Burning smudge brings in such lovely peaceful energy into your space.

As you're burning the smudge, it is even more powerful to call out to me and the Great Mystery and tell us that you love us. If you don't know what smudging is, ask a friend and they'll tell you. Burning some ceremonial sage is a good place to start. I know some two-leggeds use what are called smudge sticks too.

You can even set up an altar to me. Nothing fancy is needed. Maybe some stones and some animal figurines. That's all you need. You can light the smudge over the altar and pray to me and the Great Mystery/Creator there. If you want to get fancy, you can put some type of image of the Sacred Feminine or something like that on your altar. I do like that.

If you really want to express your love to me and be serious about it, well then it gets more complicated since your culture insists on being so disconnected from me while still living right here on me. A very big step is to wean yourself from those things that you've broken my soil or skin and dug into my rock layers or bones to get. Those things you call fossil fuels, uranium, and heavy metals.

Many of you know about this weaning need. But gosh darn it, not all of you have discovered this wisdom. Some of you, mostly two-legged males who wear those funny suits with the tight things around the neck, just have not gotten it yet. But you will—in time, you will.

Hmmm ... I know many of you who are clear about this weaning need have been marching at protests and trying to get through to those two-leggeds with the tight things around their necks. I want you to forgive yourselves for the fact that you are still using these fossil fuels, etc. The sound of all of your guilt for driving a car, or eating food that was not grown in your backyard, or whatever, is not a pleasant song to me. The last thing I want is for you to be walking around beating yourself up with a bunch of guilt in your bellies for something you were born into. It was not your decision to start drilling just a wink of time ago. That was someone else who has already died, and he had a good talking to after he passed over. Oh, yeah. His soul knows better now. So, please forgive yourselves, okay?

Now, back to the ways that you can love me. Yes, there are all of those things that you've created. What do you call them? Oh, right, chemical compounds. Some of you with very creative minds have concocted these compounds and they keep on hanging around in my soil and floating all over the world in my air and the water. I'm not sure what you were thinking. It's a violation of one of my laws for something a two-legged concocts to stick around and around and around.

A little aside. One of the things I absolutely love about the Great Mystery's universe is this thing called *entropy*. The Creator is so brilliant. This entropy, it's about how everything is always breaking down and scattering out. It's the reason that you need to keep on dusting. Entropy has scattered that dust all over, just as it makes bubbles of soap go all over the place into the air. Entropy has helped me so much with evolution. But your chemical compounds are going all over the place too thanks to entropy. I don't like this.

Some of these chemicals of yours are extremely tiny and they've been traveling through the air and in the waters, and darn it, they're making my frogs sick! I did not create frogs to be born with extra legs. And my poor fish! Some of them are being born both male and female, and this was not my design plan. Many of you two-leggeds are having a hard time making babies too. Or getting disastrously sick. You wonder why?

Others of these bunches of chemical compounds are bigger. The stuff you call plastic? They are messing up my beaches, my swamps, everywhere. My turtles are getting sick eating the plastic waste, and on and on. So ugly.

And they're killing some of my babies. Nets floating around in the ocean are trapping my whales and dolphins. You're messing things up, and I really wish you would get some common sense and stop making those things. There are wiser ways, you know.

Don't you know one of my laws is nothing lasts forever except elements and atoms? Everything goes back to my skin or bones and is used again and again. Almost every single thing is food for something else at some point in time. But somehow most of you did not learn this. I know some of your chemicals do eventually fall apart and break down, but that is only after they've messed a lot of things up.

I think I need to set up my own school to teach you how to take care of this world of mine. It will be called Mother's School. But, no, I suppose I've already created that, and it is called Earth. You are all living and breathing it, and supposed to be getting the lessons right now.

Unfortunately, your grades are not very good. At least, for most of you. And some of you are getting very bad grades. Especially those male two-leggeds who sit at those desks inside so far away from my beautiful soil and make decisions about digging into my skin and bones for your so-called fossil fuels. I have some words for those two-leggeds, but I'm going to not say them here. Nope.

But again, please don't go to that guilt place. That's really not helpful for you or me. Your culture just started out with some bad ideas not too long ago and then something called *greed* came in and you all are living with the … well, the ripple effect from those bad ideas. I hope that's a good way to put it.

Okay. Another way to love me is to go plant trees. Plant more trees. I love my trees! Talk to them as you plant them. Baby them.

They are baby trees. Make sure that they are well watered and the soil is good. Check on them. These are young living beings who need TLC. They need to be loved over time just as you do.

You know I really like this *sustainability* thing some of you are talking about. That is a wonderful way to love me! But you know, it was going on long before you all ever existed and was far beyond your two-leggeds' ideas of *sustainability*. It was and still is a planetary dance of life, and energy, and celebration. It's been a wondrous web for a long, long time. Oh, a delicious, magical, amazing web of my insects, and flowers and trees, and four-leggeds. All my beautiful four-leggeds ... and six-leggeds, and finned ones and winged ones. The list is so, so long.

Oh, there are so many ways to love me. It is hard for me to list all the ways in one message. The key is you can just start doing something today.

I guess the most important thing is to realize I am *Sacred*. I am part of the Great Mystery, just as you are too. But I am your Mother here and my whole planet is about as Sacred as you can get. You can pray to me as well as offering prayers to the Great Mystery/Creator.

I especially love it when you talk with me. All of you. I hear your prayers too. Really I do. And many of you are learning to do this. This makes my heart sing.

Okay, gotta run. Sarah, you're the best. I love you so much. Maybe next time I'll bring a joke. That would be fun!

Oh, and why don't you think of a question to ask me for our next meeting too, okay?

I love all of you!

Message 2

About the Environment, ah ... Me

Mother: Hi, Sarah! Welcome, welcome!

Sarah: Hello, Mother. It's great to see you. I've had the best week. Life is getting so much more fun. More friends are calling me up to invite me to play. And the kids at the pre-school don't stress me out these days the way that they used to. I think you might have something to do with this.

Mother: Well, perhaps. I am sending you good blessings as you go through your day-to-day activities. It's the least I can do. You are helping me so much with these messages. So, I brought you a joke today. Are you ready?

Sarah: Okay.

Mother: What bone will a dog never eat?

Sarah: I don't know. A chicken bone? I know they're not supposed to eat them. All those splinters in the bones.

Mother: No. A trombone.

Sarah did not know what to say. It was one of the worst jokes she had heard in a while. It was the type of joke that one of her four-year-olds in her pre-school might have said, except they wouldn't have known what a trom-

29

bone was. *Earth Mother was clearly amazing but her sense of a joke was a little off. But Sarah did not want to offend Mother so she decided to be supportive at least.*

Sarah: Oh, that's cute. That's funny. Thanks, Mother.

Mother: Thanks, I rather liked it myself. So, this time around, Sarah, do you have any big questions that you want to ask me?

Sarah: I definitely do. It's so terrible what is going on around the world with all the environmental destruction—destroying parts of you actually. It's so hard to have any hope about the Earth and what is going on. I know I don't need to tell you about all the horrible events. You know so much more than I do. But the radiation from Fukushima, the mercury in the fish, the GMOs in our food, the weird weather patterns and on and on … I mean, it's so hard to have any hope, or even get out of bed in the morning with this news. How can we have any positive future with all of this happening right now? I've felt such despair and have been so depressed about all of this until you and I started meeting. But still, even though my mood has gotten better, the news is just awful.

Mother: Yes, I can see how you and so many others feel such despair these days. These are very trying times. And believe me, they are trying for me also. I'm not exactly having a party right now with all of this going on. Between the contamination itself, the forests being cut down, coral reefs dying … and the way you two-leggeds are fighting, it's enough to give me a bad case of malaise.

You two-leggeds have only been around for a short period, but you've certainly wreaked some havoc. Some parts of me feel a little like the cancer you two-leggeds and four-leggeds get. But I don't get cancer. I'm so ancient that the places where there are huge strip mines or environmental contamination, such as Bhopal are just little irritating scabs I'll heal over rather quickly in geologic time. But it is going to take a long time as you two-leggeds count time.

I am 4.8 billion years old and getting that kind of age on you gives you a much greater perspective on what's happening now. All of these wounds on me will eventually heal back over, and the contamination will get buried into rock layers just as the oil deposits and uranium layers were buried many millions of years ago. I am honestly hard-wired to heal. But it's going to take a couple million years. That is certainly more than a little wink of time.

Don't get me wrong. I'm certainly not a happy camper with all of these foolish activities that are so destructive to me and all of my babies. No. So many species are gone now. Extinct. I worked for millions and millions of years to bring these species into being through evolution. It is very irritating to me that you two-leggeds have wiped out so many, so fast. I mean in the wink of an eye, gone.

(Sigh ...)

But I'm most worried about you two-leggeds. I'm worried about what is in your hearts these days. What is this sickness that has overtaken you that compels so many of you to be so blind and ignorant and, well, greedy? This makes me so sad. Very sad.

I love you all so much. You are my children. All of this evolution that I brought forth on this beautiful planet is my love at work. But somehow you've lost touch with the love. You've lost touch with me and my millions and millions of years of love. You've been taking it all for granted.

Okay, I'm starting to make you even more discouraged now, Sarah. I can see this. I'm sorry. That's not what I want to do.

So, here are some things that can help you and your friends, and others. This will help you build up hope again. I will list them for you.

Know that I'm so, so ancient that I will always heal from what is happening now. I, your Earth Mother, am not capable of dying.

Hmmm ... I take that back. When this solar system sizzles out in billions of years, I might move on from being the Caretaker of this planet to some other job in the universe. But I won't ever die. My consciousness will always exist. And I can't worry about all that's in the future. All we have is *NOW*.

For you two-leggeds, all of you can do a number of things *NOW*. Here goes:

Plant trees. Anywhere and everywhere you can. I love my Standing People, as my native peoples call trees. Wherever groups of trees are planted and nurtured they call in other species to live amongst them. Trees are very good at this and love doing it.

Have fun! Think in circles and not straight lines. Everything cycles and gets reused. A fallen tree log becomes food for mushrooms and all sorts of other critters after that tree has lain on the ground for some time. Cycles, circles. I've never designed a straight line anywhere on the planet. But you two-leggeds are a little obsessed with straight lines these days. Rather boring to me.

Go back to the wisdom of the plants instead of all the concocted chemicals that you have made up in laboratories. This never made any sense to me either. I already provided you with all the chemicals you need from plants. It's all there.

Have more fun! See the web. I don't mean the Internet. I mean the Web of Life. It's all connected.

Grow more of your own food near your homes. All of those lawns that are mowed way too often, I've never understood those. And don't even get me started on the raking of the leaves in the fall. If it is open land and does not have a forest on it, then why don't you grow food there? Put in a garden. Herbs. Flowers. Vegetables. Get some goats, chickens, or sheep. But lawns? They don't do anything for me. Especially when they are treated with your chemicals to grow only one species of grass. It's that straight thing again, I suppose. I'm into parties of species all living together. You two-leggeds call it biodiversity. The more wild parties of all sorts of critters and plants, the better. This is how I steered evolution. Wild parties of plants and animals.

Have fun! Throw a party growing the food and then cooking it together. Invite the neighbors. Have your own wild parties!

Stop breaking my skin and digging into my bones for your energy. It hurts me and just is a mess once you get it out. I'm talking about the oil, the uranium, all the heavy metals. And *fracking* for natural gas! Oh, my, fracking is the most stupid thing you two-leggeds have come up with since nuclear energy. You come up with some doozies. Putting all those chemicals in the ground to force the gas to come up is going to take me a very, very long time to clean up. Very. Why do you need so much energy anyway?

Have more fun! Think of all the ways you can use a bicycle or the wind or sun to do what electricity, or fossil fuels, provides you right now. Have bicycle parties. Take them apart and turn them into utility bikes to haul your groceries or a piece of furniture. Why not?

Hmm ... what else? Oh, yeah. Get to know your neighbors. Help your neighbors out. If they can't grow food in their yards since they've gotten elderly, ask if you can grow food there and share it with them. Have potlucks. Dinner parties with music. Cook your homegrown veggies. Preserve them. Grow gourds and use them to make new musical instruments or feeders and houses for my small winged ones. Ask your elderly neighbors to tell stories. If they're too grumpy, go ahead and be nice to them anyway. They've probably got some old wounds from some other parts of their lives and just need some love.

Did I mention have fun? Bottom line, have fun in your life! Life is meant to be an adventure and a celebration!

Oh, right. Please remember the sun. The sun has all this energy and it gifts the planet each and every day. Even when it's raining, the sun is still out there. How I love our sun. Couldn't have done all of this without the sun, you know, all this evolution. You two-leggeds can be more creative with the sun too. Some of you have been. Need to get those ideas out more. Why do you need to break into my skin and bones when you have the sun? There is the wind too. I really like those newfangled wind thingies ... what are they called? Right, turbines. I find them almost as good as something I would've come up with for evolution. Good on you for those.

Well, this list has gotten probably too long. I need to head off now. Other projects elsewhere. A Mother's work is never done.

Love you, Sarah.

Love to all of my two-leggeds. And four-leggeds ... and winged ones ... all of my beloved ones!

Message 3

I'm Not Happy

But I'm Not Dying

Mother: Hello, Sarah! Good to see you again. Yes, it is very good to see you again. I'm not sure whose turn it is to do a joke, so I'll go ahead and do one. Heard a really good joke the other day down in New Zealand. "How does a penguin build its house?"

Sarah: Hmm ... I didn't know penguins had houses. I thought they collected stones for nests.

Mother: Well, you're right. But let's pretend they make houses.

Sarah: I have no clue.

Mother: Igloos it together! Get it? Igloo ... chunks of ice!

Sarah: Oh, Mother ...! You know your jokes are kind of corny. I like them. I do. But they are on the corny side.

Mother: Yeah, I know. I think I'm partial to the corny jokes. Alright, this is actually going to be a short lesson here in the Sacred Grove and then I want to go for a little stroll with you to show you some things.

Remember, I love you all so, so much. All this evolution around you and inside of you is an act of love between me and my work and the Great Mystery's work. Please take this in. I love you all.

So, I need to set the record straight on something. I've been getting the drift that some of you two-leggeds think I'm going to die with all the environmental destruction, climate chaos, or global weirdness, as some of you call it.

I am not going to die.

Somehow you've gotten the notion that because some corners of me are being polluted with toxins or species are going extinct that I, your Earth Mother, your Earth, is going to go belly-up.

Well, first off, planets don't go belly-up. We actually don't have bellies. And that's not what we do anyway. I will be alive as your Earth Mother consciousness for as long as this solar system exists.

When the solar system finally fizzles out and Earth along with the other planets go off into stardust, then I will go and have a vacation for a couple of million years. Then I'll probably be assigned to another fledgling planet, to help nurse it along. Or I might do something else. I was assigned to this splendiferous planet way back, but my consciousness ... who I am ... may shift to being assigned to some other part of the universe later on. Way later on. But those topics are beyond the scope of this message.

So, no, I won't die. Planet Earth will not die.

However, having said all that, many of my species babies have died or are in the middle of dying or being extirpated, a funny-sounding word that you two-leggeds have come up with in English. Extinction is forever when it comes to my species babies. It took me a very long time to bring those species into existence, so I'm none too happy about seeing them disappear in a snap. No, I'm not happy about that at all.

But it does give me great hope that so many of you love me. More and more of you are growing to love me more. And seeking to restore forests, and wetlands, and helping to heal certain corners of me. We just need a whole lot more of that going on and a lot less destruction, such as trees taken down and wetlands filled in.

You know I'm working on an evolutionary development for you two-leggeds, but it's just taking too long. It's something to do with an anti-greed vaccine, but I'm having a hard time getting the pharmaceuticals to support the research.

Just kidding! I don't hang out with the pharmaceutical companies. I love the idea of an anti-greed vaccine, though.

Okay, so I promised you a short walk in the forest, Sarah. Let's go!

Whereupon Mother grabbed Sarah's hand, yanked her out of her wooden chair, and headed straight to the far corner of the Sacred Grove and into the surrounding woods.

Sarah, I want to take you outside the grove where we're going to lie on our bellies and peer at the forest floor. In this body, I guess I do have a belly. How funny. Anyhow, we're going to gently scratch around the forest duff a little, and I'm going to show you a few things.

Mother magically pulled out a beautiful wool blanket of many colors that was about six feet by eight feet from a hidden pocket in her outer skirt. Apologizing profusely to all the insects large and small on the forest floor there, she carefully spread the blanket out for them to lie on.

Sarah, so few of you do this. So few of you actually take the time to lie still on the ground and just watch the life around you. Especially on the forest floor. This makes me sad. I love it when you two-leggeds show interest in the animal and plant life around you. I especially love it when you talk with them, and give them love. They deserve love just as much as any two-legged or four-legged. Trees love to be loved up. They all adore that.

So, here. Look. See that little millipede? Watch their tiny little legs. So many of them. I was so proud of myself when I designed them. All those little legs. So cute.

And here's a grub under this small piece of wood. Nice and fat and juicy, but we'll put him back since it would be nice if he grew into an adult beetle unharmed. There's a small wasp over there. The kind that doesn't sting, don't worry. And under this small piece of wood are all sorts of little critters. I honestly can't remember all their names in this very moment. I have so many babies and I know about all of them, but don't ask me to list all the ones that are here right now. Some are so tiny you can't see them. I can see them though. There are bacteria. Insect eggs. Plant spores. Mycorrhizae. Oh, so many, many babies, right here in just one square inch.

And if we dig in the soil a little with this stick ... need to move some leaf litter ... let's see. There're some more beetles, different types. A pill-bug. Oh, there are billions and billions of bacteria, microbes, microscopic life here, just under this very blanket we're lying on. Plus, you know what? Your two-legged scientists have not even discovered all of them! Right here in your country, in a forest that is only about thirty miles from some two-leggeds with all of those degrees at one of those university places, there are species they still don't know about. I rather like it that I still have so many secrets.

Let's look at the dirt. Most of you think dirt, or soil, is dead. Oh, no. Not at all. It's so alive and beautiful, and everything in it is always feeding and being food for something else. Oh, yes, it's such a dance of life, even here in the dirt.

Sarah, there will always be some wild corners like this alive on the planet. Always. I'm making sure of this.

Oh, I have so many, many secrets that the scientists have not discovered. So many. Most of these they won't discover since their lens on the world and science is so limited.

Oh, but now I'm getting bugs up my skirt! They're starting to crawl up on the blanket.

I love you guys too, but off my skirt! Don't get all caught up there. No!

Sarah, I think that covers the message for the day. I don't want to have to kill any of these buglies but some of them bite and I need to shake out my skirts and gather up my lovely pocket blanket.

We'll see you next time. Mr. Tufts is waiting for you inside the Secret Grove again to lead you to your trail.

I love you! Love all of you!

Bring a good joke next time!

Message 4

About Dying & Living

Mother: Sarah, good to see you! Once again we meet. I am loving, loving these visits. Hmmm ... I think it is your turn again for a joke. Or even any sort of silliness. I absolutely love silliness.

Sarah: Okay, Mother. I've been playing around with limerick writing. I memorized one to share with you. Here goes. It's called *The Banana Limerick.*

> Bananas have three sections,
> For many a predilection.
> Yummy for the tummy,
> Don't eat when strumming.
> I prefer them over national elections.

Mother: Oh, Sarah, I love that! You probably didn't know this but bananas are one of my most favorite designs in all my evolution work. The way they grow hanging in bunches from the banana trees—I love how that worked out. How you two-leggeds hold them and unpeel them in sections. Even the apes do that. It just makes me feel all tickled inside when I watch all of you enjoy them. Plus the fun foods that you cook up with them too. So, so creative!

Hmmm ... as for national elections. Not my favorite thing at all. At all. All the mud-slinging. There are days when I feel like giving them some real mud-slinging. But I don't ... I don't. I restrain myself.

Okay, Sarah, you can choose a topic today again. What would that be?

Sarah: Mother, I would like to know about death and dying. What really happens when you die?

Mother: Oh, this will be fun. Good question. Though I'd rather be calling this message about "Dying and Living."

Sarah, when you die, you only die to this dimension, this physicality on Earth. When your body gives up the ghost—oh, those poor sad ghosts, never mind them right now—then your soul-body travels to another spiritual dimension and it all starts over again. You still exist in your soul-body then. You are just not on Earth, my glorious planet, anymore. You have moved on to another spiritual plane.

It's a rather beautiful thing, dying, actually. Though most of you two-leggeds are so afraid of it. That makes me so sad.

Some of you two-leggeds are only starting to realize there are so many dimensions to the universe. When you die, there are spiritual beings that help you cross over to another dimension. When you get to that gathering place for souls who have just passed on, there is a big party. Loved ones you knew in life greet you and there is a big, big celebration. Of course, time does not mean anything over there, so the celebration lasts as long as it lasts.

When the festivities are over, you are guided to the Library of Souls to view your particular book. Some call this the Akashic Records. Your soul has a book for all of the lifetimes that you've lived. Everyone has a book. In that book are the records of all you did and said, your kindnesses, your not-so-kind moments. You review your life there and are given the opportunity to consider what you might do better next time. Then, after a period, usually about thirty years or so, you come back. You're born into another body here.

But you've never really *died, died,* as in *gone, gone.*

You see, the Great Mystery is not only a Mystery with a capital "M" but is also the Great Recycler with a capital "R." Your soul just goes and goes. What is it that you two-leggeds say about an *Energizer Bunny?* It just keeps on going and going. Though there aren't any batteries in your soul to give out.

Your soul-body can get sort of dented, though, and need fixing. Many times life on the physical plane can be a school of hard knocks, and your soul-body can get damaged when you've experienced a lot of trauma. There are gifted healers who walk among you as two-leggeds, and they can help you recover from current or ancient trauma. It's so lovely when you find a good healer and you feel so spanking beautiful and whole after visiting one of them. It may take a couple of visits though.

I love my healers so much, since they help to bring my two-leggeds' soul-bodies back into a place of good alignment and wholeness. The song that you put out after this alignment is so sweet. It's actually healing for me too, when this happens. Your song is in closer alignment with my song of love and joy and wholeness. It's so lovely. So very lovely. It's good when you two-leggeds can find one of these healers ... good for you and good for me.

Most of you don't know this, but it's actually a huge treat for you as a soul to be living in the physical on this planet. Eating a cherry, tasting that sweetness. Jumping into a cold river or lake and feeling your body tingle all over with aliveness. You can do this only when you are physical on this planet. You can't do these things when you're in the spiritual realms.

Each of you was born with memories from previous lifetimes embedded in your soul. This is what motivates you to seek out certain hobbies or careers. Perhaps you were a musician beforehand, a gifted one. Child prodigies are children who were extremely gifted at whatever skill or aptitude they had in a previous lifetime. Those soul memories are not lost.

Your soul memories can also speak to some of the deepest challenges in your current lifetime. Maybe you died of an abortion in a previous lifetime because the ancient herbal knowledge that could have prevented your pregnancy was hard to access, and you had to seek out an abortion from someone unskilled in a dirty room in a dark alley. Something that traumatic becomes a soul memory in this lifetime, and you might not be so inclined to have a child since that horrific death memory is still there within you. You might even develop health issues over time in your womb-space because of the soul trauma. This is when you could seek out a gifted healer since this type of soul memory is a wound in your soul-body.

Or maybe you cut someone's hand off in a past life and then are born without a hand in this lifetime. That happens. Or you're terrified to get into a boat or even to swim because you drowned in a past life. So many different experiences that each of you carry into each lifetime. Rather fascinating, actually.

If you were completely healed and your soul-bodies were singing as brightly as they could, you would love your physicality and sensuality. That is part of the great gift of being born here in a body. You get to enjoy this body for as long as you are in it. Sometimes you have pains and health issues, and other times you are experiencing the gloriousness of your body with a partner or alone. I know the aches and pains do get a little harder when you get older. It's part of the beautiful process of being alive.

Just as my dolphin children love their physicality and rub all over each other and make love all the time since it is such a joyful act for them, you two-leggeds could be doing this too. You could be enjoying your bodies and the incredible deliciousness of being in one that is capable of making love and tingling all over again and again. Responsibly though. Responsibly.

Many of you two-leggeds have been taught that it is a shameful thing to enjoy your bodies. You've gotten all warped about this and made the act of bringing yourself to a full bodily wave of tingles wrong. This just baffles me so much. Why would anyone ever want to stop you from enjoying your body, this beautiful body that has been made possible through my work and love, all of my evolution, along with the Great Mystery's love too?

Some of these so-called rules that some of you learn in those buildings where you talk more about God or the Great Mystery than anywhere else really are not helpful.

Now, I do think some of the rules taught in those buildings are smart and good. This is true. It is good to learn how to forgive. It is not good to kill other two-leggeds willy-nilly. It's good to be kind. Not good to steal.

But the rules about that one day, the Sabbath Day, being the only holy day in the week ... I just don't get this. *Every* day is a holy day. Every day is a day to be close to the Creator and me, your Earth Mother. Every day and every moment is a time to consider the Sacredness of your being alive as a soul-body here on my glorious, incredibly fun and delicious planet. I mean we have peaches and chocolate and fresh bananas here. This planet is amazingly delicious!

You know, what is it that you two-leggeds call it? The Ten Commandments? Next time, Sarah, I will give you Earth Mother's Commandments. Though I'm not sure if it will be ten. I have to give this some thought between now and then.

Okay, I've got to run. You know it's still a lovely day. I hope you

45

go for a long walk in the woods after we part here in the Sacred Grove.

Love you!

Love all of you so much!

Message 5

Mother's Thirteen Commandments

Mother: Hello, Sarah! I like your hiking clothes today. A mighty smart-looking rain-parka you're wearing. But you don't need to worry about it raining on us in our Sacred Grove this afternoon. I've made arrangements about that. I know it looks ominous, but you should be able to get back to your box on wheels, what you call your car, before the skies open up.

Sarah: Thanks, Mother. I was rather worried about these clouds.

Mother: Oh, don't be worried. You'll be fine. Okay, so my turn for the joke. I can't remember where I heard this one. How did the panda who misplaced his dinner feel?

Sarah: Ahhh... Hungry?

Mother: He was bamboozled! Get it? Bamboo—zled. Bamboo ...

Sarah: Yes, I get it. I get it. Hmmm ... Mother, no offense or anything, but I think I need to get you a good joke book. I mean a really good one.

Mother: You don't like my jokes? I think they're good. I like them. Anyhow, enough of jokes for now. So the last time we met I promised you I would come up with my own set of Commandments. Not

47

the same ones that many two-leggeds read and pray on from that black book. These are *Mother's Commandments*. There are thirteen of them. Along with some precepts or whatever you want to call the other list. I like the word *precepts* myself.

So I will say them slowly so you can record them. Here goes:

Mother's Thirteen Commandments plus Precepts

1. I, Earth Mother, gave the planet a song. Know that you are part of this song as one in the vast web of life, no greater, no less. All that you do affects the song, for better or for worse.

2. Your thoughts, both positive and negative, affect the song as much as your actions.

3. Everything has consciousness, the stones, plants, even mountains, rivers and oceans—all join in the song. Know that your thoughts and actions are registered in the song and affect the stones, plants, mountains and all, for better or for worse.

4. Developing silence of the mind and from this place— deep gratitude is one of the most positive things you can do for Mother and all others in the song, especially those very sensitive and intelligent ones such as the whales and the dolphins.

5. Fear that comes from your head is an illusion. Fear that comes from your instincts is not. Learning to discern between the two will help in stilling your mind and being in the moment.

6. The song is most harmonious within an energy dance of love, compassion, tenderness, patience and coopera-tion. It is good to learn this dance with all beings with whom you interact, whether two-legged, four-legged,

winged or finned ones, standing ones (trees), or stone people.

7. Come to understand your shadow self and make bringing it to consciousness to heal it part of the dance and celebration.

8. It is all just energy—money, time, your job, your play, your love. Choose to make it as positive as possible and lose the illusion of fear with this energy dynamic.

9. Love is the foremost energy. Mother loves you. You all evolved from love. Evolution is an act of love.

10. Know that perfection is an illusion. You are all the most beloved and delightfully flawed beings as two-leggeds and that is how it is meant to be—and it makes you all the more lovable.

11. Know and honor your Mother as you honor your Creator. And if you want to put an icon of me on an altar, that's fun. But any other graven images are not needed.

12. Have fun! Life is a celebration! Life is an adventure!

13. The more you celebrate life, the more you help your Mother to heal all over the planet, and encourage the whales and dolphins and all others in the song to sing more harmoniously with you!

And here are my *precepts:*

- Touch Mother everyday. Touch her skin, her earth. Let her healing energy come into you to calm you and heal you.

- Do not gouge Mother's skin or break into her bones.

- Do not create compounds that will last longer than the very short-term out in nature.

- Honor the forests and replant trees.
- Honor the wetlands and restore them.
- Do not waste.
- Clean up your rooms. Big and small.
- Live in community. All are part of the community. Everyone's needs should be taken care of by the community. Share.
- Listen with an open heart.
- Speak with an open heart.
- Be lean of judgment and speech.
- Be open to the mystery that lies in people and the world around you.
- Be compassionate with yourself.

Now, I'll explain a little bit to help out here. I know that some of your smartest scientists have started to write about what they called Quantum Physics. I call it Sacred Energy, but never mind that. So everything has an energy field to it and there is a vibrational hum to these fields, but not too many of you can pick them up. But these fields exist and some of your two-legged equipment can pick them up.

I, as Earth Mother, also have a vibrational tone or hum. This is not the sound of an earthquake or lightning storm but a consistent hum. It's not any human sound. Far from it. Your two-legged ears can't hear it. It would be nice to think I could join a chorus with it, but now that I'm thinking about it, my tone is part of the universal chorus and the smaller group of humming planets from the solar system along with all the other planets, stars, asteroids, black holes, etc. in the universe. Not all of our sounds are pleasant to everyone but that's okay.

There is also a collective vibration or set of sound waves that all of you two-leggeds give off. It used to be a lovely sound for thousands and thousands of years. But more recently, your sound has gotten rather ... well ... hard to take. There is so much anger and hatred and violence in it. It makes me so sad. Plus, it is really hurting the dolphins and whales, not to mention the other species children here—this sound that all of you two-leggeds are making together.

Now don't get me wrong. Some of you, my beloved two-leggeds, are putting out a beautiful song as individuals. When some of you gather to meditate and still your minds, this is a beautiful sound for me. Or when there is a lovely drumming circle in the woods and you are all feeling so joyful with the beating of the drums together on the ground. Oh, that's a lovely, lovely vibration that makes me so happy.

But not too many of you do that. Nor do you sing very often. You are all so serious. Then you go and watch movies of such violence, or play war videogames. I don't understand this at all.

You all need to lighten up so much! Your life is meant to be one of celebration, singing, drumming, dancing. Growing food together. Singing to the plants to help them grow. Drumming to the moon. Sharing all of these beautiful foods together so everyone has food.

Oh, I could go on and on. Definitely you need to have shelter and clothes and food, but to be so unhappy about making that happen in your lives; how sad this is, for you and for me. For all the species. There is just so, so much fear in your lives.

This pains me and makes your song kind of hard to take. I love you all so much. I really do. This is perplexing to me that your society has taken the song to this place.

So, it's getting on and the clouds are looking more threatening and I can't stave off the rain forever. So let's continue this conversation next time.

Thank you, Sarah ... Thank you. I love you.

I love all of you buckets and buckets, oceans and oceans!

Message 6

About Love

Mother: Hello, Sarah! Great to see you again! Oh, but you look rather glum this afternoon. What is wrong?

Sarah: Mother, I know it was my turn for a joke. But I'm just not in a good mood for a joke. Please, Mother, tell me about love. Daniel left me about seven weeks ago so he could travel the world. I miss him so. Why is love so painful? Why can't we love another person without so much heartbreak?

Mother: Oh, Sarah, my love. No worries. We don't have to do a joke. Love is very hard for my two-leggeds, isn't it? Here, come over closer to me and let me put my hand on your heart to help it heal.

Sarah went over to Mother's chair in the Sacred Grove, and Mother put her hand gently on Sarah's heart chakra and held it there for about thirty seconds. She finally lifted it slowly and gave Sarah a deep warm smile. Once again Sarah felt a shimmering warmth in her heart, similar to Mother's gift of healing on the day they first met.

Mother: Sarah, just let the energy I gave you sink in. Take some slow deep breaths and just feel whatever is coming up for you. I just gave your heart some healing energy to help you release the pain that had gotten trapped there. You can go back to your chair. You should feel better soon.

Yes, love. Love is such a beautiful and powerful part of your existence, isn't it? It's not like most of my beloved creatures who have such strong instincts to mate and then just walk away from each other afterwards. I know some of you two-leggeds do that too, and it is certainly a beautiful way to celebrate your physicality without attachments. But you need to take care to do this with care and sensitivity.

Then there are some of my creatures such as my swans and even black vultures who mate for life and are heartbroken when their mate dies before them. I feel for them, yet that is what these species chose to do way back when they were first evolving. They carry a great heart pain, too, since most of them never find another mate afterwards.

As a Planetary Caretaker I cannot experience that type of romantic love. It's not as if I can go date other planets and procreate little baby planets. Though the idea rather tickles me.

I know your two-legged romantic love can be so complicated and yet, so simple. For me, as your Earth Mother, true love is a way for you two-leggeds to bring more cherished children into the world. They've been blessed with a divine love from the love in your hearts in the moment of their conception. This is a very potent love that will carry with each child forever.

Love is a spiritual journey. Many of you forget this. The journey is never over, and it is a glorious one since your lover is your highest spiritual teacher. They will push you and poke you and tear your heart and spirit open again and again to encourage you to learn about where you need to grow within yourself. It is a journey of learning kindness, compassion and forgiveness and so much more.

If you doubt love or fear that you have none, know that this is never true. You are *always* loved by myself, your Earth Mother, and by the Creator. Our hope is that you can also discover the love within that you can give to yourself.

Yes, there are so many types of love. Romantic love is only one type. Please know that the Great Mystery and I do not care if you are a man loving a man or a woman loving a woman or a man and a woman loving each other. All we care about is the quality of the love there, and how your hearts and spirits are growing with this love. Ultimately the love you feel there is connecting with the Divine in each other. You can help each other develop your individual God-spaces in a powerful way.

There is the love of a parent toward their child. Or two old friends who have known each other for a long time. Or siblings in a family. Or even a grandparent and a grandchild. Where there is that heart warmth for each other, there is love. My heart sings to see these different types of love.

The mystics know about another love too, the love for the Divine. They bathe and bask in this as you all bask in the arms of your lovers. Yet everyone can learn to give love to the Creator and me, your Mother. The Creator and I are always sending you love, all the time. But this does not mean that you automatically send it back to us. This is *your* choice.

Ah, yes. Free will.

We do yearn for this love from you since it helps you and your species evolve on my gorgeous planet Earth. When you send this out to us, it is a divine energy that supports me and all the other beings on the planet so, so much, beyond what I can tell you here. But it is up to you to give us that love back, or not.

You can love the plants in your garden and tell them so. You can love the trees in your yard or at the park. You can work with them from a place of prayer. When you see the hawk flying overhead, you can send that hawk love. You are all my children and I do so love all of you. You are all gloriously connected in the dancing web of life on my planet.

As for romantic love, this is a beautiful path that can be a treacherous one too. It is treacherous since so many of you have not grown in your hearts to the extent you could. So you get caught up with attachment, and needs, and ego, and control, and those are cavernous pits that many of you fall into without realizing it.

Do not love out of fear. Love is not owning another two-legged. Love is cherishing and honoring that other two-legged so that they too can grow in their divine love to Creator and me. For the stronger their divine love, the more they will see you as part of the Divine too. And your love, like a passionflower vine with endless and endless blooms of such breathtaking beauty, is a never-ending journey of growth and bliss, and, yes, sometimes even sorrow and pain. But when you feed it by connecting into the divine love from me and from the Creator, oh, it's so delightful for me. And you. And even the Great Mystery.

Not all romantic love is meant to last forever, though. Sometimes there are soul contracts between you and another two-legged, when you come together to learn and open your hearts and spiritual awarenesses to a certain place. Most times you offer a healing to the other. Then you are each meant to walk away to continue your paths elsewhere.

These are a part of a greater soul contract that each of you agreed to before you were born, when you were still in spirit and preparing to come back here for another incarnation on Earth. Each of you developed such a contract for your work here as a two-legged. Part of that contract involves some of the other beings you will meet along your path, and the ways in which you will help each other.

There are a number of things you agreed to do, but most of those are beyond the scope of this message.

If you are suffering from heartbreak, do not curse that other two-legged. You never owned them to begin with. Look into your heart and your mind and see all that they have taught you. Has that two-legged encouraged you to grow spiritually? Have they brought you to a place of deeper compassion in your being? How else have they helped you to grow emotionally?

Celebrate that this other two-legged helped you grow and learn, the one you feel took a hatchet to your heart. And then give that tremendous and awful sorrow and pain to me, your Mother. And to Creator. Give it to us. We don't want this to fester in you forever. That makes you sour and hurtful. Let it go and give it to us. We can heal anything if you allow us to heal it. But you must give it to us. Some of you use that expression: "Let Go, Let God." Yes, but don't forget your Mother also. You can give it to me, too.

Okay, I've got some other meetings elsewhere. Some of the Thunderbeings are holding a council and I need to go and moderate. They can be so uppity. I've got to try to calm things down.

I love you, Sarah!

I love all of you in ways that you can never know. Such beautiful, incredible ways!

Message 7

About Conflict & Soul-Woundedness

Mother: Sarah, it's another lovely day here! I'm so glad the weather is nice for our visit today. Then again, I did arrange for that. Never mind. Okay, I don't know if you found a joke but I heard one the other day that I love. Here goes: What is the difference between snowmen and snowwomen?

Sarah: Gosh, Mother. I have no clue. Their noses?

Mother: No ... *SNOWBALLS!*

Sarah: I like that one! That's funny. You're getting better, Mother. That's a goodie.

Mother: Well, I think my sense of humor is not quite like a two-leggeds', but that's okay. I'm trying here. Okay, now let's get on with our message today. You can ask me another question.

Sarah: Okay. I have a good one. Mother, why is there so much conflict on Earth? Why are people fighting each other so much? Some of these people are even suicide bombers. Why is this?

Mother: Oh, Sarah. Yes. There is too much conflict around my beautiful Earth. I have been watching this grow and grow, and it saddens me so much. So very much.

I love you all so much. You have no idea how much I love you. If only all of you could take this love in and hold it within you, maybe there would be less conflict.

You see, the source of all this conflict is that you two-leggeds have developed a sickness in your soul. A soul-woundedness, really. Most of you have it. Not all. My beloved two-leggeds who still live very deep in the jungles, away from all those ugly wires that carry what you call electricity, they don't have this soul-woundedness. Even some of you who live within those wires that crisscross most of my continents don't have this sickness. Some were born without it and others have learned to heal from it in their earthwalk.

It makes my heart sing that some of you have been healing from this sickness. You are the ones who are planting gardens and remembering to honor me. You help your communities grow more gardens where there is so much sadness in your cities. In some areas where buildings have burned down or been abandoned, the rubble has been scraped away and now there are some really nice tomatoes growing there along with other veggies. I've been trying to grow some gardens there also, where the buildings have crumbled. Yet I like your gardens a lot too. I like how they are making some people happier in the cities. Most two-leggeds don't appreciate my garden designs these days anyway.

You healing ones have been doing so many things that give me such joy.

But most of you still carry this awful woundedness. All of this aggression. This suffering because someone is dominating another one. Some of you two-leggeds even buy and sell other two-leggeds! What is that about? I had hoped you all would get that out of your system by now, but not so.

These suicide bombers and others who plot big schemes of killing, both people and animals—what makes them do that is a sadly advanced form of the soul-woundedness that I'm talking about here. They have gotten too disconnected from me, their Mother, and from the Great Mystery too. Their anger and hatred has gotten so deeply knotted into their souls in those groups, those clusters of two-leggeds, that they even say in their buildings where they come to pray that the Creator or Great Mystery wants them to be a suicide bomber. Well, the Great Mystery I know would never want any two-legged or any other being to act in that way.

It would be a good time for that soul who is the Christ Consciousness to come back to my beautiful planet. Oh, such a beautiful soul with such purity and spiritual wisdom. Somehow many of you have learned some weird things about this soul. When I'm hoping this soul will come back, I'm not talking about the "Saved" business where some of you will rise up to "Heaven" and others will go to "Hell" based on "Jesus Christ coming back."

No, I'm talking about the deeply, deeply compassionate healer and teacher of great spiritual truths who knows how to bring peace back into two-leggeds' hearts. This teacher does not distinguish between one two-legged and another with their capacity to be healed.

It's never made sense to me why those two-leggeds are so eager to leave this magnificent planet of mine to be "Saved." I've worked for a couple of billion years to make this planet as amazing as it is, with the help of the Great Mystery and others, of course. Most of this has been great fun, all the evolution stuff.

But some of these two-leggeds don't like it here enough, I guess. It baffles me that they can't see that my baby, my planet, is a part of Heaven, right here under their very feet and all around them. If they spent more time away from the messes most of these cities have become, they'd see this. I'd hope so, at least! But they spend more time in buildings than out in the forests or by the ocean. They, too, think that the Creator is only found in buildings. That is definitely something I've never understood.

So much of this just completely baffles me. I've never been able to get through to so many of them. I guess that's why you're here, Sarah. It used to be that all of you knew me and honored me and what I do, and there was very little soul-woundedness. Used to be ...

I know, I just know my planet will return to being heavenly too. I'm very determined about this. If I have anything to do with this, it will get back there and it will be even better. Some of you two-leggeds are seeing this and working on it. I adore, just adore each and every one of you who are working on this. And playing on this too.

Frankly, you all work too much anyway. You need to play more, and that would help me out. I don't mean play inside and exchange that stuff you call 'money' for other stuff that you don't really need. That's another thing that baffles me.

Go play in the woods. Or the rivers. Go sing and dance along the ocean. And pick up trash while you're at it.

As for the soul-woundedness, some of you two-leggeds need to learn and live more forgiveness! If there was a way that I could get the clouds to rain forgiveness-enhanced water down all over the planet, I would. Hmmm ... not a bad idea. I wonder if I can do that? Wonder what it would taste like? Ah ... chocolate! I might see if this is possible.

All of you need to hug each other more too.

But about the Christ Consciousness—you know I can't give away any secrets. But some native peoples have been talking about how this soul is already here again. Some think that this soul has come back as a woman. That would suit me fine. But I'm not going to give away any secrets.

Ha! I can't do that!

Okay, gotta run, Sarah. Hugs! See you next week! Oh ... bring a good joke too!

I love you!

I love all of my beloved two-leggeds. Yes, I do ...! And four-leggeds, and all the rest of my delightful critters ... and stones and rivers, such a list! All of you!

Message 8

About Facebook & Twit-Twitting

Mother: So, here we are again. Sarah, so nice to be with you again. I just love you so much and appreciate your doing this—meeting me here for these messages, and then sharing them out there in the world. Hmmm .... I think it's your turn for a joke. Do you have a good one for me?

Sarah: Well, Mother, I knew you'd ask. So here it is: How long do chickens work?

Mother: Hmmm ... as long as they live?

Sarah: Around the cluck!

Mother: That's very cute. Very cute. Okay, next time it's my turn for the joke. Now, let's move on to our message today. I can't be here overly long. Bear with me, but I'm going to choose the topic today. I'd like to talk about Facebook and Twitter and twit-twitting on those medium and small-sized boxes most of you spend far too much time in front of. I'm referring to your computers and cell phones and those not-very-smart phones.

I know you're starting to realize I can be a little opinionated.

65

When you are 4.8 billion years old, you're allowed to get a little opinionated. I do try to keep my mind open. Don't get me wrong. Believe it or not, I am still continuing to learn. You two-leggeds continue to teach me about a few things. The Great Mystery is still continuing to share some new things with me. It's all good.

But. But. I've started to learn more about Facebook, this thing on your so-called Internet.

First of all, it's a fascinating thing. Most of my two-legged children with access to those boxes called computers are connecting via electrons through cables and wires and even through sound waves. It's very interesting, and I suppose mostly a good thing. Some of it ... but not all. You see, I'm still trying to sort this out.

There is good sharing of ideas and news, I suppose.

I love that some of you have been making new friends across the world. Though I'm not sure what kind of friendships these really are. Maybe they are really more like warmish contacts. Not cold contacts. Those would be more dead, I guess. No, those of you active on the Internet are very much alive, blipping messages and short comments so fast that it's spinning my energetic grids in a funny, weird way.

You see, that's part of what's hard for me. I know one of your religions talks about the 'monkey mind.' This is that hyperactive mind of a two-legged who can't still his or her thoughts to calm him or herself deeply. I know you know what I'm talking about. Facebook and Twitter are like a global collective monkey mind, all jittery and nervous, that is ON all day and all night. But it's not *my* mind that is all monkeyish. It's all your minds combined into one huge mishmash that circles the planet in a frenetic pace, while I'm left in the middle looking for planetary-sized sedatives to take. But the Great Mystery does not hand those out.

My gosh, the gossiping! The games. The trolling of total strangers' photos and messages. The quick responses without thinking much about what you are saying. The blip this, blip that. It's a miracle any of you can focus on anything after spending time there. I think most ants have a longer attention span than most of you do after being online.

Then there is the carping. The negative comments. Some hateful comments. Some fights. You all don't even know each other, and you're allowing yourselves to get all worked up over silly comments?

Don't you know all this is energy? Your thoughts are energy. The electrons shooting these messages are energy. What a dreadful song of dancing electrons you are putting out there, most of the time.

Well, not all of the time. This is true. Sometimes there is beauty and wisdom, and beautiful connections between some of my two-leggeds there, two-leggeds who wish to help me, your Mother. And some good jokes. I like the jokes a lot. Sometimes there are some very positive wavelengths that come through and this makes me happy. But those are so far and few between.

As for Twitter. Oh my. That makes Facebook look like real conversations, the way that you all tweet this and tweet that so fast. The energy behind these tweets is not so helpful in my work as your planetary caretaker. Do other two-leggeds really need to know all the stuff that you're typing in there so fast? How did you all get so trivial and gossipy?

Then there is text messaging. It's like Twitter to me. Many of you walk around holding those mini-box phones and typing in little messages. I fear you will get hit by a truck doing that. Plus, you're missing out on the bird songs, the hawk that might be flying overhead or the geese migrating.

Maybe you all could take more breaks from those things? It used to be that two-leggeds would knit or crochet, or even do macramé in their spare time. Or whittle things. Or even read a book. Be productive. Whatever happened to those things?

I wish that I could shut the whole system—Facebook, Twitter, cell-phone mini-boxes, even the Internet—down for the weekends, so I could have a break. Many of you take weekends away from your jobs, but Planetary Caretakers can't take much of a break. Especially not me these days.

It would make me so happy if all of you took weekends off from the twitting, Facebooking, and even turned your computers off and spent time outside with me. And with my plants, four-leggeds, winged ones ... all of my other creatures. I think you all have forgotten most of them.

There is this entire world that I have worked very hard on, very hard, just outside your doors—and most of you have tuned me out of your lives. It makes me so sad how much of my planet is paved over, dumped on, dug up, etc. Most of you have forgotten all the critters that existed there where you now drive or live or play golf. Naming your streets after the animals and trees that have disappeared just does not count.

If all the two-leggeds who used Facebook and Twitter and cell-phones spent just as much time outside gardening or planting trees or picking up garbage as you spent on these gizmos, then maybe I would not complain so much.

I have not even brought up videogames, the ones where you are killing each other in these artificial worlds! Since when did you all get so focused on killing? Some of those games are even blowing up dolphins! Whatever happened to games outside where you honed your ability to hunt? Or to collect herbs for healing?

You don't hear when I complain anyway. Well, some of you can hear. Very, very few. And those aren't the ones doing all the messaging or twitting.

I love you all. I really do. I just want to drop some sense into you these days and remind you where you came from. Remind you how all my plants and other creatures live side by side with you, but you mostly ignore them.

A mother's heart can get heavy. Very heavy. (Sigh ...) But I find hope that many two-leggeds will be reading these messages once you get them out, Sarah.

What I would love to see all of you doing instead are activities such as playing the drum. Or singing. Or dancing. That would make me so happy. Or doing all three together outside on the bare ground, in bare feet. Ohhh ... I love the way that it feels when my two-leggeds do that.

Okay, enough for now. I know, I'm opinionated. But if you all only knew how all of this feels to me ... I know you'd have migraines if you were me.

I love you ... all of you!

Now please turn off those contraptions!

So much love to you all!

Message 9

About Gratitude

Mother: Hi, Sarah! Do you know that we've now been meeting for nine weeks here in the Sacred Grove? This is so much fun!

Sarah: Yeah, that's pretty amazing. The time has flown by.

Mother: Indeed it has. So I've got a joke today. It's a knock-knock joke. Are you ready?

Sarah: Hmmm ... Do I have a choice? Just kidding, Mother. Of course I'm ready.

Mother: Knock knock!

Sarah: Who's there?

Mother: Howl!

Sarah: Howl who?

Mother: Howl you know unless you open the door?!

Sarah: Oy! Mother! Your jokes ... they are so ... precious. Yes, precious is the word. I really need to get you that joke book. I do. You are so funny.

Mother: Well, I try. I try. Okay, so today I want to talk about gratitude. So many spiritual two-leggeds speak about this. I think I need to talk about it too. I suspect I might have a slightly different angle on it.

71

Honestly, your culture is really not so good at gratitude. Most of you seem to have forgotten how amazing and magical it is to even be alive. To be living in a two-legged body.

Now some of you are aware of this. And some of you practice gratitude a lot. This is a good thing. But only some. Very few of you.

But geezy-peezy, when was the last time any of you said thank you to the trees around you? Not only are the Standing People—which the wiser ones on this planet call trees—cut down cruelly to make things like thank-you cards, or toilet paper, but all the animals and plants that live in those forests are also destroyed with this—what you call "clear-cutting." And so few of you ever think of thanking them for all they've given you.

I mean, don't most of you study this about trees in school? They give you oxygen. They give you firewood. They give you wood to build your homes, shade to cool you in the summer outside ... I don't think I need to list all of the things trees give you. Not to mention all that they provide for so, so many other species. But when was the last time you thanked them?

Same goes for the water, the fish. The animals. Oh, you don't want to get me started about gratitude toward the animals that you eat. You do need to eat—I understand this—but what is it with the way you treat these animals, where they stand all day in their feces and are given chemicals to keep them from dying there in their feces? How insane is that? Then you turn around and eat that meat with the chemicals in it? I mean, that's crazy!

Ay-yi-yi! I really wonder about many of you and your common sense. I coordinated this planet's evolution so animals that live on the land eat plants growing fresh from the ground, or bushes or trees. The plan is that you two-leggeds who eat meat would go and hunt them. Or you can keep some of the plant-eating animals inside fences when they get used to you, or you herd them. That's all fine.

And I know you eat plants too. But to have these poor cows or chickens or turkeys or pigs standing in manure day in and day out, and then being dosed with chemicals that you've come up with—this just does not make any sense to me. And you wonder why so many of you are sick ... but that's another conversation.

I wish all of you understood how amazing it is to be alive on this planet. I love this planet so much and I love you all so much. All the trees and flowers and bugs. Oh, my precious buglies. I love all of you. The fish, the teeny-tinies that you use microscopes to see. I love all of them. I even like leeches. They're kind of cute in their funny slimy way. They all have a place here on my beautiful planet. They eat things. Things eat them. It all works out.

But you all have forgotten what a blessing it is to be alive. I'm going to repeat that. And say it louder. "*You all have forgotten how amazing it is to even be alive here on this planet I take care of!*"

All you seem to do these days is take and take and take and take ... I think I could say take a million times over again. I've been around a long time, you know. All of you two-leggeds are such newcomers. But troublesome ones most of you've become in the last wink of time, from my view on things.

So it would be really nice for you all to start giving too. *Giving.* Saying thank you to that tree outside would be a good start. Or giving the tree some good manure too. Not the manure from the places where the cows stand all day. That manure is a little scary.

Or saying thank you to the water coming out of your tap. Or to the lakes and rivers and aquifers that you even *have* water coming out of the tap. Or to the water where the fish you ate last night lived. Or the fish. The crab. The lobster. Whatever you ate. Even the parsley on the plate that most of you don't touch in the restaurants. You can thank that too. I have no clue why you don't eat that parsley. It is usually the healthiest thing on the plate for you to eat anyway.

Please be careful how many of these fish you catch though. I am concerned about how many of them you are eating and their ability to survive all your taking. Oh, don't even get me started on how many of my species babies you all have wiped out so far. I don't want to go there in this very moment ... makes me want to cuss really loud, and I don't think you're ready for the types of cusswords that Mother can say!

Hmmm ... you know, you can even thank me sometimes too. Directly, I mean. You can offer tobacco to me. Or cornmeal. Doing prayers outside and laying little piles of good clean tobacco or cornmeal at the base of trees is an old native way of honoring me, your Mother. If you don't have tobacco, you can gift me with a small amount of whatever food you've got there. The whole idea is giving back. Prayers count a great deal too.

Okay. There you have it about gratitude.

Oh, oops. Not quite finished. There is something else here. When you all start expressing gratitude more, and really *feeling* it, you would be amazed at how wonderful that feels. For you and for me. For all the beings on this planet. When you two-leggeds start saying thank you from a place of really feeling it deep in your hearts and your bellies, oh ... it's like the way you feel when you eat really good chocolate for me. All nice and happy and slightly buzzing. For all of you to be feeling gratitude and expressing it out loud is like amazing energetic chocolate for me on my level.

You see, this beautiful energy of gratitude just starts to move through your rooms and houses, to other two-leggeds around you, and four-leggeds, to the ground under your house, to the trees and the birds and the flowers. Oh, it's such a sweet, positive energy. And I love it. It tickles me so and makes me happy. So happy!

I love to be tickled!

I'm going to give you some homework. The next time you eat, try to eat in silence. Even if you are with someone else, both of you can eat silently. Focus on every bite silently. Chew it slowly. Say thank you to each bite and to the food on your plate, each forkful of food. Try that. Try it several times. See what happens. Enjoy the food. Enjoy what I've created on this planet for you to eat.

Now off with you. I've got other things to do. I'm a busy Mother, you know.

I love you ...!

Every single one of you, small and big and short and tall and teeny-tiny to big-big ... all of you!

Message 10

About Cooperation not Competition

Mother: Hello, Sarah ... Hello, Sarah. So delightful to be together again, isn't it?

Sarah: Yes, Mother. It was a very nice hike up here again. It amazes me how it never rains up here when we meet. Some of these afternoons it's been rainy in the city but it always stops when I hit the trail to meet Mr. Tufts and then join you here in the Sacred Grove. I know you've been helping the weather a little.

Mother: Ah, Sarah. Yes, I do what I can. It would be a shame to get all wet in the Sacred Grove while we meet. Today, today ... I would love if you'd share about something you're very grateful for, instead of a joke. Make my heart sing a little.

Sarah: Let me think for a moment.

[long pause]

I've been writing up your messages and sharing them with friends, and people are really responding to them. Most love them. This has inspired me to do some other creative writing. I've been working on some other pieces to get published too. All this writing makes me feel so alive and passionate. I love it.

Mother: Hearing that makes me feel so wonderful! One, that people are liking the messages so much, and two, that you are doing something that makes you so happy. I love it when my two-leggeds find their soul-work and they are so joyous. That's just beautiful and tickles me. Really tickles me and makes my heart sing. When you are all singing with joy in your lives, it helps me sing too.

So, today I want to talk about a funny idea that many of you two-leggeds have gotten into your heads. Actually one of many funny ideas, but never mind that.

It's the idea that this beautiful planet that I've nurtured along for all of these millions and millions of years is based on *competition*. Somehow you have concocted the notion that all my lovely species are having a battle fighting over the minerals in the soil or the sunlight in the forest—all the time.

This is not true. What's happening, and has been happening since I nurtured those first cells along in evolution, is that most of my glorious species are *cooperating* most of the time. But you have seen the world through a lens of *competitiveness* for so long that it's hard for you to understand this.

That two-legged called Darwin—he was a very hard-working man and traveled all over in those beautiful ships that were so silent and clean. I miss them. Anyhow, he traveled to so many various nooks and crannies of the continents and collected so many parts of plants and animals. He even studied earthworms. Fascinating man. But his mind was working so fast, and he got so caught up in his ideas of "survival of the fittest," and "dog eat dog," etc., that there was no way I could get through to him that he was completely missing the truth in front of him. Just like almost everyone else in his culture, he was not going to listen to me, his Earth Mother.

What most of you don't realize is that all of the beautiful four-leggeds and standing ones, the finned ones, the winged ones, they all know it's a dance of life. They know they need to find food and they need to make more babies. They also know they need to eat some living beings and they are lunch for other beings. It's a dance of being completely in the moment for them.

You see, I designed it so they would be able to live with all of their special ways and be in the gloriously *huge* web of life. I'm constantly tweaking this and that so one species can do a little better or be a little smarter. Maybe add extra antennae, or longer ones, to a bug. Or a fish might evolve a slightly more elongated fin to swim faster. There are a billion improvements to be made all the time. You should see my "To-Do" list. It's rather long. But I'm used to it.

When a lion catches that sickly or weak gazelle on the Serengeti, the herd knows in advance that one gazelle is not meant to live a long life. The lion knows it needs to eat. They accept these things and know it is part of the dance. This is not to say they don't grieve though.

Oh, my elephants, they grieve so when one of them dies. I love them so much, and I grieve with them: they are so wise and gentle and fine. I especially love their trunks and their feet. Some of my finer design moments. I guess maybe there are a lot of fine design moments. But I don't want to toot my horn, really. It's just my job to love all of my beings here and to keep on nudging evolution along.

As I was saying, so many of my four-leggeds grieve. Most of you have no idea how emotional or how intelligent most of these other four-leggeds, winged ones, and others are.

But I'm getting off track here. So, yes. *Cooperation.* The dance.

In the forest, trees are communicating and sharing all those lovely minerals and organic stuff all the time. But you two-leggeds can't see it and most of you have assumed that trees are just dumb lumber standing. But they are not dumb at all. Some of you have learned how to communicate with trees and you know how intelligent and emotional they can be.

Trees grieve too. They grieve when one of them dies, especially the very ancient ones among them. They know their elders and respect them greatly. Some of you feel when trees grieve, I know.

You see, trees thrive on living in community. They have a vast network of roots and root hairs. Fungi live on the roots and act as transporters and telephones all at the same time, sharing each tree's minerals and information with the others. This phone/chemical exchange can go from tree to tree to tree, all underground, for long distances.

At the same time, trees are chatting back and forth with each other, sharing the news in their energy fields. Trees do chat by ways other than their roots. When one is sick, they all know it. They try to help the other trees when they fall sick by collectively communicating and sharing information on how to create an immunity to the disease that has come in. I help them with that, but they take the initiative. They're very smart.

When some two-legged walks into a forest with a chainsaw, believe me, every tree in that forest knows it, even if they are miles away. Trees are not dumb. They especially don't like chainsaws and how mindlessly they are used. There is never any offering, no seeking permission, no honoring the Sacredness of the trees when the chainsaws come in. It makes my heart break, how many small and large chainsaws are being used all the time all over my lovely planet. Oh, my trees ... my standing people. And all the other four-leggeds, six-leggeds, bird nests, all those beings in those forests that are lost, just lost, when a forest is cut.

In a healthy forest where chainsaws are far away (thank goodness), trees are cooperating by sharing their spaces with their beautiful leaves, so everyone gets enough sunlight. They are always helping each other and they know it's a dance for light in the forest. So the lower branches in most of my tree babies have larger leaves than the upper branches. They will send out a branch in a certain direction to take advantage of a gap with more light. But it's not as if they are fighting and cursing each other as some of you two-leggeds have been known to do at rowdy events with too much fermented drink in your bodies. They know they are a community and dancing together to live together.

Of course, there are times when a seed falls at the base of a tree and starts to germinate. This can make it kind of tough for the larger tree. But I assure you, there are intelligences there that negotiate and work it all out peacefully. Many times the seedling becomes like a lover to the original tree. It can be quite sweet to see how they grow together and develop a bond. However, most of you are oblivious to these intelligences.

The biggest challenge to me is that you two-leggeds keep on moving four-leggeds, six-leggeds, and viruses, seeds and other critters around the world. A couple of beetles that are supposed to be living in Asia, since that's where I put them, show up in New Jersey since you shipped them there. Those beetles get out with their mates and before you know it, or I even know it, they are munching on all sorts of things and there is nothing much munching on them. Or you take rabbits to Australia. Or mongoose to Hawaii. The list goes on and on. Kudzu to the south of the United States. Eventually they all get loose. Of course they get loose. Or seeds are scattered by birds or animals or the wind. That's what all my critters want—to be free. Wouldn't you want to be free too?

This is when competition comes in, since these plants or four-leggeds or six-leggeds, etc., don't have anything munching on them for the most part, they run rampant. My poor native species don't have much of a chance. I know you know what I'm talking about. My plants—they want to help you. They do. For thousands of years, when medicine two-leggeds have gone out for walks, the plants have whispered wisdom to them about which ones can help heal different ailments and how and when to use their leaves, stems, blossoms or roots. That is how the original herbal wisdom was shared. The plants talked with the medicine two-leggeds.

But plants only want to help when they are honored for their Sacredness. They will speak only to those who have learned humility and learned how to listen. Those who give blessings, tobacco, cornmeal, or other gifts to me in ceremony are the ones who generally learn how to listen the best. I need to see that you are willing to be humble and open and patient in order for me to wake up those abilities in you so you can listen. This is the way. Of course some of you have been born with these abilities. You are so delightful to me.

For those who learn these ways and seek to be in relationship with me, your Mother, I can help you so much. So much. But you need to want this relationship with me, and show your love to me.

It used to be that all my two-leggeds were in close relationship with me. There would be dreaming women who would come together and dream together in the same tents or caves or wherever they lived. These women were particularly gifted, and many dreamed the same things. They would discuss their dreams since these were messages from Spirit to help their village.

Sometimes their dreams were from the overarching Spirit of the deer or gazelles or other wild four-leggeds, and that Spirit would tell them where to send the men for the hunt the next day. The men would then go off and find a herd exactly as the women described it. There would be one weak deer or gazelle as the women described and that would be food for the village for the next few days. This is the dance between Spirit, the two-leggeds, and the four-leggeds who were hunted. Some of my two-leggeds still live this way. But not many.

There were very close relationships between my two-leggeds and the four-leggeds and plants. They all danced together to help each other live and make babies. It was all so beautiful. Yes. I miss that.

I know these days can return and be even better. I know you two-leggeds have the capacity to be wiser and more connected with me.

I know you, Sarah, with your pure heart—you could learn how to live in this way in very close relationship with me and all my loved beings. All my beloveds.

So, that's it for today. I have to go and check on an earthquake that's taking shape in the South Pacific. It's threatening to break and I want to make sure that it's as harmless as possible. As if an earthquake could be harmless. But I try.

One of these next times, let's talk about how my two-leggeds might be living in closer connection more and with greater love for me. That would be most fun. Let's do a dream journey together, Sarah. Oh, I'm getting excited thinking about it.

Yes! Let's do a dream journey together soon!

So much love to you, all of you!

Love, love, love!

Message 11

To My Sons

Mother: Hi, Sarah. Wow, we're into Message Eleven. We're certainly getting to be good buddies. Yes.

Sarah: Yeah. I'm loving these meetings with you. They are so much fun.

Mother: Me, too. So, Sarah, this is going to be a different type of message today, and I forgot to bring a joke. And I'm eager just to launch into it. I'd like to send a message to the male two-leggeds. Here goes:

My sons ... my two-legged sons. I love you so, so much. Yet most of the time these days I just want to shake some of you. Not all of you but some of you. Maybe many of you.

How did you get so disconnected from me and from the path of wisdom? It used to be that you knew about the wise ways. All of you did. You knew how to tune into the land and where to grow the food, and when and where to let the land rest. You did the prayers to help your food grow, and knew how to hunt so the weaker animals would be killed and the herd would stay strong.

There was a time when you understood the mystery and strength of the women, the ones who gave birth to you and the ones whom you lay next to at night. You listened to the dreaming women who would send you to the right areas for hunting. You would care for the children when the women would gather for their moon ceremonies. You became the nurturers during those times of the month so that you would learn some of the ways of women, to help you stay humble and balanced in your roles as partners in your family and village. Just as the women stayed humble in their roles.

Something happened several thousand years ago. This goes back to before you were recording your two-legged history. I guess it was a number of things that happened. But the balance that was there for so long between men and women two-leggeds started to disappear.

The temples to the Goddess—*to me*—were destroyed and the women had to flee and so many were raped and assaulted. My priestesses, my daughters ... oh, if I could cry, my tears would have filled several planets of oceans then, as I watched so many of my two-legged daughters being forced to hide their gifts, their healing wisdom and strengths. Many were tortured and lost their lives. This went on for centuries. Waves of torturing and killing. So much cruelty as some of you male two-leggeds began to fear and hate what the women could do. Such sadness in me then and now for the abuses that still continue. I never understood it. Still don't understand it.

I know there are many of you, my sons, who honor your two-legged women. You see their gifts and support them in their struggles and joys as mothers and caregivers, juggling what they do within the family with their work outside your homes. They are asked to do so much.

Many of you live in places around the world where the women collect water and haul firewood for miles to help ensure that you have water and cooked food. It is not that you don't work also, but

I watch my two-legged women give and give and yet receive so little respect in return.

I just don't know what I can do other than give Sarah these messages to share. I love you all so much.

But those meetings where there are only men two-leggeds, wearing those tight things around their necks, sitting around a table making decisions without asking any women to offer wisdom and insights, just do not make sense to me. There have been too many of these types of meetings.

Observing those meetings—there have been so many of them—does help me understand how so many of my forests could be destroyed and wetlands filled, and how my skin and bones could be cut into so you could scrape or drill out things that I put in there long ago. These things were never meant to be used by you two-leggeds—the oil and uranium and other things that you have been scraping out of me for purposes that I have yet to quite understand.

Don't get me wrong. I do understand energy. I understand that very well. I just don't understand why you all could not see the wisdom of playing with energy in other ways. The sun shines on me every day. There is so much energy there. I tapped it for the plants so that life could really flourish here. You have barely started to tap it. Some of you have developed some very clever ways to work with energy, such as that clever two-legged called Tesla, but then the ideas just vanish. Gone. Baffles me.

My native two-leggeds knew not to break my skin. I think some of them tried to tell some of you with the lighter skins, but there was no listening.

So now you've cut into me in too, too many places. I will heal. I know I will. But I'm not so sure about how this has mucked up the way it rains and snows and how the winds blow, *and* what this means for all my children.

I mean, I'd like to see all of these wounds healed with some very good eco-Band-Aids and all that. But you see, my Thunderbeings and elementals and too many others to list out loud, they're quite frustrated and angry with you two-leggeds. I try to calm them down before there is a hurricane or tornado, but they won't listen to me anymore. They tell me there are too many two-leggeds anyway. They think that you've gotten too disconnected from me to understand or repair what you've done, so there is no point in being compassionate and gentle anymore. They used to be more compassionate.

There is the issue of all this carbon dioxide in the atmosphere too. What a mess. Many of you already know there is too much and are trying to change things. You're working hard to stop new drilling and scraping projects and other such nonsense. You're focusing on using less energy, too. I'm very grateful for those who understand this.

Oh, it's all gotten too complicated now. My mind just spins with how complicated it has all gotten in your two-legged world. All the bickering between your different groups makes it hard for me. Your collective song is so harsh now. I know I've talked about this before.

Then there are the things you have created to kill other people. It just seems you have completely lost your minds! You keep on coming up with bigger and fancier ways to kill other two-leggeds you have never met, over in some other part of the world. It just looks to me like many of these things are being built and used so that some of you, very few of you, can find more stuff below my skin and in my bones for you to drill up and use.

It's not that I don't understand war. I do. When one of you two-leggeds, ah ... generally a male these days ... gets out of line and starts to take over another country, it makes sense to stop that two-legged and his armies. I do get sad about how many of you die, yet I can understand that type of war. I am very puzzled, though, at decisions that were made to start some of the more recent fighting around the planet. They've created an awful energetic stink from my point of view.

Forgive me for sounding so grumpy and giving this whole list of things you men two-leggeds have been doing. I just don't understand. In this teeny, tiny bit of time you've ravaged a lot of corners of me and it's going to take me a bit of time, a good bit of time to clean this up. Not to mention all my babies that have gone. Zip. Extinct. Disappeared forever. I know I'm repeating myself, but ...

I don't know. Maybe I'm just not in the right mood today to be giving any messages to anyone. I'm just not in a good mood. When I see some of my daughter two-leggeds being forced to wear big black bags over their bodies and being beaten for having their ankles exposed. Others are kidnapped so young and forced to have paid sex—more like paid rape. Then there are the daughters who are never born because the mothers are forced to abort them, or who are killed after birth because a boy two-legged is more prized than a girl.

You are all my children. I love all of you so much. So much. You are supposed to be equals. You are supposed to be caring and respecting each other equally. Women and men are supposed to be making decisions together on how to run the village and bring food in to feed the families. There are women's gifts and men's gifts—all the various and different ways you are blessed in your masculine and feminine two-legged bodies and minds and spirits. You're supposed to be blending these gifts together.

The crux of it for me is that most of you two-legged men have forgotten the *Sacredness*. Your Sacredness. How your Sacredness is tied in with my—your Earth Mother's—Sacredness. Not to mention the Sacredness of your women two-leggeds. Plus the rest of the web of life's Sacredness.

You have forgotten the mystery. The power and wisdom of humility in knowing your place in this beautiful planet. The great intelligence of the Creature Teachers—all the four-leggeds around you. You

89

have forgotten all of these things and more. So much more.

Yet ... some of you are relearning this. Especially many of you younger ones. You are reaching out and learning to touch me with reverence again. You're planting trees. You're finding ways to honor me. You're trying to get other male two-leggeds to listen to you and hear the newfound wisdom you're discovering by learning my ways and my mystery. You are even apologizing to me. I hear some of these apologies and it makes my heart sing.

Those of you who are doing this give me hope. I don't want to see all of you disappear. I worked too hard and for too long to create a planet here, an amazing planet so you could come into being through evolution. I don't want to see you all go through some silly set of actions that might take you all out. I don't see this happening anyway. But there are times when I worry. I worry. Those nuclear plants that you all have built ... they really were not the wisest idea, you know. (Sigh ...)

But, yes, some of you give me hope. I stay with that most of the time. That hope.

I think that's all I want to say right now. So much more I could vent about. But I just don't think it's worth it. You get my drift.

Now, I need to go and do something fun. I think I might go play with some otters and then check out what the dolphins are doing in the South Pacific. Those dolphins know how to have fun! I love hanging out with them a lot.

There are also some incredibly cute chimpanzee babies in some different corners. I just love being with the chimpanzee babies. They are so adorable and make me feel all tickled inside when I watch them.

So, Sarah, you know I really, really appreciate your taking these messages. This one was a heavy one to listen to, I know. Thank you for taking all of these good notes.

I love you so much.

I love all of you so, so much. Even you male two-leggeds. I do still love you!

Message 12

To My Daughters

Mother: Sarah, hello again. Today is a special day. A very special day. Today is the day I give my message out to all of my daughters, my female two-leggeds.

Sarah: Okay. That sounds good to me.

Mother: Yes. And you, Sarah, are a very special daughter to me for all you are doing with these messages. Very special. I love you so much.

Sarah: Oh, Mother, I am so humbled and honored to be able to help you with this. I still don't know why you've chosen me but I'm happy to do it. More than happy. This has been great fun and it's helped me in all the other parts of my life too. I feel so much more positive about everything in my life. Even when I got a parking ticket the other day, I just shrugged it off. I never could have done that before. Thanks, Mother. I think this is because of you and all the beautiful energy you've been giving me.

Mother: Sarah, I'm so grateful for all you are doing. So very grateful. Well, here is my message to my daughters.

How I love you so, all of my daughters! And those who remember me and offer prayers to me, I love you the most.

But the way you've been treated and continue to be treated—how this breaks my heart.

What are these big black bags that some of you wear? I can't even see your eyes nor your beautiful hair. Some of you have been treated like cows and even sold like cows. I love my cows, too, but you as two-leggeds were never meant to be treated like that by another two-legged.

Oh, and the rapings, the hittings, the abuse. All my daughters in your so-called prisons. Then there are the men who collect you like pets in a zoo.

You don't pray to me anymore, most of you. You don't remember your Mother.

Oh, my daughters, I used to gather with you when you would bleed with the moon. That was our special bonding time, when the women would come together away from the men. I was there listening and slipping wisdom to one of the elders in the tent to help guide you and connect you to me and each other more.

But now almost all of you are too frenetic. Too busy. You sit in front of your TV or computer boxes inside or hold those cellphone boxes to your heads when you're walking.

Some of you even use them when you are driving in the boxes on wheels. I think you must have a death wish, some of you. This is a sickness I don't understand.

I love you so much, my daughters. I do see that many of you are waking up and stepping into your power. But do not be fooled by the illusion of the stuff you call money. Some of you are very gifted at collecting it. Good on you.

But to hold onto this money and keep it to yourself will only make you sick in your heart. You are holding onto energy that needs to move for you to stay healthy and for other two-leggeds around you to stay healthy.

I have seen you get sick in your souls and hearts and do things that are dark because of the fear associated with this money. This makes me sad, for I don't want any of my daughters to be dark. But some of you scare me with your darkness. Even me. Your jealousies, pettiness, gossiping. How manipulative some of you have gotten. And worse. Some of you have done some very heinous things. This makes me very sad. You have forgotten so much.

I miss the temples that existed for so long where you would pray to me. I miss the blessings, the propitiations, many of you would offer me. Some of you were my priestesses. Oh, how you made my big old Earthy heart sing. How you prayed to me and taught the younger women also. You sang songs and danced. Oh, you danced and danced and brought such joy to me and the whole planet. All of the animals and plants would sing with you. You probably did not know this. Very few of you knew this.

So few of you know this now: whenever you sing to me and drum to me, all the four-leggeds, the stone people, the finned ones, winged ones, and standing ones sing with you too. Your songs help them grow more vibrant, more beautiful.

But now almost all of you are so disconnected, so distant from me in your hearts. You plant your seeds and forget to sing to them. You walk on top of me heedlessly, with your spiked heels, not blessing the ground with your feet as you once did. You wear your clothes and paint your faces and forget I am the one who gifted you with your beauty and adornments.

You have forgotten our connection and so the healing energies within you—the Earthy, healing energies all of you carry—are blocked. Just as the money energy some of you possess is blocked too.

You have forgotten it is all energy and the key to energy is to keep it moving. A river flows always and will eventually break through dams over time. Nothing is supposed to be static and held trapped here on my wondrous planet. Nothing. Not two-leggeds, not four-leggeds. Not rivers.

There is the *chi* flowing along meridians in your bodies. This is energy. And there is chi in the planet, my chi. Just as the rivers and oceans are all my blood, there are energetic chi lines that help keep me balanced across my skin and bones. Yet your mining, highways and electrical grid block my energy flow.

What you have in your body, I have also across my planetary body. What you don't realize is that this energy is all love. In some places it travels more densely, a denser love current.

Why would you ever want to block love?

This holding onto energy within you and in your lives—this is actually hurting me. It hurts me that you hold onto what you call "wealth" and don't take care of your hungry sisters and brothers with this extra energy. Some are so hungry and abused and wounded.

Many of you carry such pain within you because your bodies, your hearts, your souls have been so abused. You need to find healing.

Please, for me and all your sisters, walk barefoot on my brown soil, and my grass and forest floors, and give me your pain, your sorrow. Send it right down to me through your wombspace, your legs. Let your tears water me. I love your tears when I know you are letting go of your sorrow.

I know this sorrow. I do. Sorrow for all of my daughters and me and all the wounds across my body.

Call on me to hold you. When you are alone and feeling despair, you can ask me to wrap my love around you like a blanket. I will come as soon as you call.

Scream your pain out, if need be. Dance like mad women if this can take you to a place of less rage and more calm within yourself. Get a punching bag. I wish there was a punching bag my size because I could sure use it right now.

Oh, daughters, do you know how much I love you? I have always loved you. To have watched over the past few thousand years as you've lost your temples and needed to suppress your overt love for me—this has been so painful for me.

You have such magic within you. All of you. Magic to share your blood with me. Magic to create children within you, with the help of a man two-legged's sperm. Magic of your Earth connection and spirit that is so linked with me. Your men two-leggeds don't have this. Only you women two-leggeds. You can remember this magic within you if you try. It is time to remember. This will help not only with your healing, but also my healing as Earth Mother.

Come back to me, daughters. I miss your love, your songs and dances and blessings to me. I miss your powerful gratitude and ceremonies. I miss your being connected to me.

Oh, how I love you. How I love you!

Message 13

About a Joyful Future

Mother: Sarah, Sarah ... Sarah. I am so loving these meetings with you in the Sacred Grove. You don't know how much I look forward to them every week. It is so much fun to be chatting with you and sharing these messages. I did not tell you this before, but I'd been trying to find the right two-legged to be my messenger for a number of years. You were the one who kept on surfacing. So I kept an eye on you until it felt like the right time to appear to you. You are a very special two-legged, so pure of heart and intention. And you've always loved me. I know this.

Sarah: Gosh, Mother, those are such kind words. I'm not sure if I deserve all of that. I don't feel that special at all. As a matter of fact, I had the hardest time getting up this morning because I offended another teacher at work yesterday. It was by mistake and I felt really awful about it.

Mother: Sarah, love, you are a flawed two-legged just like every other two-legged and so lovable. Don't fret about what happened at work. You did not intend to be mean. There are two-leggeds out there who actually enjoy being mean. That's not you. You are a beautiful person. You are—inside and out. Plus, you've always been deeply connected to me. From the moment you were a young girl running around outside playing in the woods and fields outside your family's home.

Sarah: I never thought about it that way. I guess I have been.

Mother: Yes. Yes, indeed. So, this meeting today is going to be different. I'm going to take you on a journey. A journey into the future. This is going to be fun. What I want you to do is to come over here and scootch next to me here on this small bench. I'm going to hold your hand and off we'll go! Don't worry, we'll be safe.

Sarah got up from her wooden chair and squeezed in beside Mother on the bench where Mother was sitting. The space was so tight that Sarah and Mother's sides were pressed together. Sarah wanted to just snuggle right into Mother but resisted the temptation. She knew Mother wanted her to stay alert and present.

Okay, Sarah, I'm going to hold your hand and you just close your eyes and trust me. We're going to go on a wonderful journey! I want you just to observe and I'll explain things as we go, okay?

Before Sarah knew it, she was transported out of her body into a dream state that was more than just dreaming. Mother was next to her, grasping her hand as they zoomed through the air. They quickly left the forest, and before Sarah knew it, they were flying over very high mountains with glaciers that extended for a very long way. They swooped over forested valleys that sparkled with streams and rivers coursing through them and over more mountains. In one valley an eagle flew close and parallel to them. Sarah could feel its piercing gaze as they flew together. Then the eagle soared off. Hawks circled below them at several points. It felt as if they were flying across the world. But it was a different world.

Finally they arrived at a large valley with several villages dotting it. Sarah could see the chimney smoke from high up as she and Mother made a silent circle over one village. Mother guided them to the ground

*on the outskirts of that village, beyond a pasture of cows and sheep.
Goats grazed in another nearby field while chickens clucked next to a
set of gardens behind several homes.*

Mother: Sarah, we can stand here and observe this village. They
can't see us. They can't even hear us. We have traveled to the future
here and are in a different dimension from theirs. I want you to observe these two-leggeds and tell me what you notice. I know you can
see they are living very differently from the way you live in your apartment in the city. Or the way other two-leggeds live outside the city,
in those areas where all the houses look like little boxes.

Sarah: Yes, that is so true. Their homes are so simple and they are
all round and seem to be made out of ... is that woven material over
wood? And how interesting that they've been able to make curved
glass windows. Their clothes are more muted colors, none of the really bright reds or yellows or oranges that we have now. What I'm
really noticing is how happy everyone looks. The children are running around, playing a game with sticks and what looks like hol-
lowed gourds. I can't figure the game out, but their laughter is so
infectious. Oh, look! One of the children is running this way!

Mother: Do not worry, daughter, this little boy can't see us. He'll
run right by us and will never know that we're here.

*The young boy ran within three feet of Sarah and right past her to grab
some more sticks and then returned to the other children close to one of
the homes.*

Sarah: Mother, I think I see lights inside one of the homes? Could
this be possible? I don't see any electrical lines outside and yet it
looks like a lamp inside?

Mother: Yes, Sarah, they do have lamps that work. But they've
gotten smarter and don't need to have an electrical grid based on
breaking atoms or my precious coal layers to provide the electricity.
Every home has a technology that creates electricity out of a vortex

box in one side of the home. I can't explain it exactly but they've been able to create these systems that naturally return to the soil after they stop working. They are so clean and silent and beautiful. I love them. These vortex boxes power their lights, their fans, their cold food storage, just about anything they need that requires energy.

I love what they are doing in these villages. They don't rely on any materials from my skin and bones. They use the trees and plants and animal parts and their labs create beautiful things that all break down in time in a lovely way. Nothing toxic like the things your culture creates now. When they go out in the forest, they work with such reverence and kindness with the plant beings. It's so beautiful. And it's so peaceful here. These two-leggeds have learned from the mistakes of your time to leave the stuff in my bones—my rock layers—alone. Everything they are doing is coming from what they are finding in the woods and valley around them.

Let me share more with you about these villages, about aspects of them that are hard for you to see from here. These two-leggeds are very sensitive. Most of them talk psychically with each other all the time. They are very empathic too, and are constantly communicating with the plants that grow around their homes, their vegetables and flowers, as well as with their four-legged companions, the dogs, cats, sheep, etc. They recognize they are in relationship on the same level with all their four-leggeds.

But it's not as if these two-leggeds chat all the time. Their minds are much more still than the minds of the two-leggeds in your culture. They are able to sit with a calm mind and tune into nature intelligences from miles away. They know when rainstorms are coming several days in advance, by standing outside and listening and feeling. Their more gifted ones are particularly able to do this. They are powerful healers and very, very wise souls.

There are no prisons here, Sarah. No jails even. Certainly there are some who struggle and sometimes violate the village codes. But instead of being sent to a jail, they are assigned to be with a gifted one to be healed. The gifted ones, when they need a break because they are exhausted from their healing and spiritual work, go on retreat to a sacred cluster of guesthouses along the edge of the forest way over to the north. There is a big spring that bubbles out of the rocks near the guesthouses. My energy is very powerful in that place, and the healers go there to replenish themselves and tune into the wisdom of the spring and rocks. The village people know that the space is sacred for the gifted ones only.

Ceremonies are held here often. Ceremony for the plants, the gardens, the harvest, the moons. When a baby is born. When someone passes over. When someone goes through a major healing and is born into a new phase in their life. There are ceremonies for all of these events. I love their ceremonies since there is so much fun and love and dancing, singing, drumming—all of it. It's such a joy for me to come and visit them here. You see, I can travel here into the future anytime I want. I do this often to help me stay hopeful in the midst of all you two-leggeds are going through at this time.

One thing this village does *not* have is people who have the greed sickness. That was healed several generations ago. Whenever anyone starts to show any sign of hoarding or not sharing, they are immediately asked to go and sit with one of the gifted ones for some healings and teachings. What a relief to me that the greed sickness no longer prevails here.

Yes, everything is shared. Food is shared. Homes are even shared at times when someone is in need. No one goes hungry. No one is lacking. Everyone knows the community is watching out for them to make sure they get what they need—food, or warm blankets, or even hugs. They build homes together, and it's amazing the systems they have. These homes go up fast with everyone cooperating and singing while they're working. Sometimes they tell jokes too. Even corny ones. I love those corny jokes, as you know.

And I love how the elders are so active. They live with their children and grandchildren. They watch the young ones when the parents are gardening or working in the village craft centers. The smiles on these grandparents' faces. Oh, it makes me all tickled inside, seeing how happy they are. And you know what? These elders live until they are into their 120's or so.

When an elder or anyone takes sick, they go to another part of the village, a cluster of cottages where they are treated by special gifted ones with the most powerful healing abilities and knowledge of herbs. It's all done with such love and kindness. So beautiful.

Sure, there are times when some two-legged might get upset or angry or have a bad day, but these bursts of emotion are short-lived since they are surrounded by such love. They are supported in healing through their moment's pain so quickly.

When there are decisions to be made that involve the whole village, they come together in a circle with specially selected women and men, elders and teenagers. All viewpoints are heard and weighed. These two-leggeds are good listeners since their minds are so still. It's fun to watch these meetings and see how they move from voice to voice to take all the wisdom into a sacred container to distill it all into decisions that serve them all.

What is most remarkable is how they perceive time. They trust there is time for everything and that all will be taken care of in the right time. That great fear of a limited resource called *time* does not exist there. Some of them, the gifted ones, even know how to bend time.

Sarah, this is the future. Your culture, believe it or not, is evolving toward this.

I only wish that I could snap my fingers and take you there in a millisecond. But your culture has to work through its growing pains to finally arrive at this place, these beautiful sets of villages in clusters around the planet.

Come, it's time for us return to the Sacred Grove now.

Before Sarah knew it they were back in the Sacred Grove. She settled back into her body as if she had been in a dream. Yet part of her yearned to fly some more and visit more of these magical villages of the future. And soar with the eagle over the pristine valleys. It was so beautiful and peaceful.

Mother: Sarah, I have just taken you to see the future. I need you to write about these villages. I need you to share what you have just seen so the two-leggeds of today can see that glimmer of potential and hope beyond the chaos that is rampant in your world today. I know it's my world too, but your lives are so short. This is really your two-legged world that is cracking open to birth a new world. That is what your rather crazed wink in time is going through right now. My world, my planet is going to make it just fine through this very, very short-term bumpiness. I'm continuing to tweak some species with their next evolutionary phase. I'll be working with the Thunderbeings and elementals. And the earthquakes and volcanoes. I'm fine, though taking a little bruising—it is true.

The hardest challenge for all of you today is finding hope in the midst of the turbulence. Sarah, this is one of the most important messages for you to share. You two-leggeds need the hope.

Know that each person who reads your messages, Sarah, will be seeded with this vision of hope. They will be the ones to take leadership in a variety of ways to help bring this future in reality. There will be many who won't read your messages, and they won't be seeded. But that is okay. Not everyone is meant to be seeded.

I will help you get these messages out. I'll be working in mysterious ways to help you get these published and out into people's hands. Don't worry about that. I know you've never written a book before. Don't worry.

One more thing ... Sarah, this will be our last message for now. I need you to work on polishing all the messages I've given you and sending them off to be published. Once you've done that, there may be more messages later. I need you to stay focused on printing these up and spreading the seeds of hope for the future. The seeds of love and connection with me, for the future.

Sarah: Oh, Mother, please don't stop the messages while I'm working on the book and polishing these other ones up! Please! I've come to love these visits with you in the Sacred Grove so much. I've loved Mr. Tufts and how he waits for me on the trail to bring me here and take me back. I can't imagine stopping these meetings.

Mother: Sarah, I will always be with you. I've always been with you—since you were born, actually. Don't worry. I'll visit you in your dreams. There is a good chance that we'll have more meetings here too. Mr. Tufts is not planning to retire from his job. He has already informed me of that. But right now you need to focus on getting this book out. Now, don't cry. Remember, I will always be with you. Always.

Mother stood up and pulled Sarah to her and held her as Sarah started sobbing. She held Sarah for a long time until Sarah calmed down, exhaling softly into Mother's chest for a while. Then she gently pulled back from Sarah and looked at her.

Mother: Sarah, I have just seeded you and healed your heart more deeply than before. You are a messenger for the future. For the unborn two-leggeds of the future. For all of my children of the future, four-legged children, six-legged, finned ones, winged ones, standing ones, all of them. Your work with these messages is important. Here, let me give you one more hug. Then I need to be off. But I will visit you in your dreams. I promise I will. Often.

Mother gave Sarah one more deep embrace and then touched her hand to Sarah's heart again.

Mother: Such a beautiful pure soul you are, Sarah. I love you so much.

Okay, I've got to head off. Remember, I will be visiting you. So much love, so much love to you. And to all of my two-leggeds. So much love!

With a final twinkle in her eye, Mother turned, walked to the edge of the Sacred Grove and disappeared. Once again, Mr. Tufts magically appeared at Sarah's feet to take her back to the trail in the forest. Sarah was surprised at how uplifted she felt. She thought she'd feel despairing about leaving Mother and the Sacred Grove, not knowing if she'd ever come back again. Instead, she felt buoyant and excited and started to brainstorm about how she would schedule her time to get the messages together quickly into book form.

Before she knew it she was at the trail. Mr. Tufts actually gave her a little wink before he turned and disappeared too.

Alone, Sarah hiked back to her car, pondering on her dreamtime and how she knew Mother would be visiting her there. Maybe Mother might even bring some more corny jokes to dreamtime. Sarah smiled at that thought. She'd look forward to more of Mother's jokes—as bad as they could be—even in her dreams. Now on to the book!

MARE CROMWELL

APOLOGIES

With apologies to all of the six-leggeds, eight-leggeds, many-leggeds, those who slither and those who crawl, as well as the ondines, salamanders, sylphs, devas, fauns, dryads, gnomes, fairies, brownies and oversouls, Landkeepers, nature entities—all of you. For the sake of brevity, I could not mention every one of you in this story.

And deep gratitude to the whales who are the record-keepers who report back to Earth Mother, Divine Mother, and to the dolphins who called me to the beach in June of 2012 to hear the beginning of these messages. Thank you for encouraging me to listen to your call, for all of us to listen to the call of Mother, so that we may serve her to help our beautiful planet and ourselves evolve to that world described in the last chapter.

ACKNOWLEDGEMENTS

Katherine Carter, beloved, beloved Katherine, my 100 year old friend with the warmest kitchen and bountiful canned food, who asked me when the book was coming out for at least eight years.

Phila Hoopes, amazing sister-friend, and editor extraordinaire;

Margaret Pennock and Marcia Wiley, deep friends from long-time Ann Arbor days;

Diane Davis and her lodge community of great compassion and Spirit;

Hillary Banachowski and Kat Clark, gorgeous (former) sirens of Linganore;

David Hazard, writing coach extraordinaire, who steered me all winter and spring and gracefully accepted that Spirit wanted to start coaching come July;

Dr. Norman Dy and Dr. Alexandra Welzel for their humor and openness.

The brilliant minds and beautiful hearts of FaceTribe, for their support and incredible insights and intelligence;

My parents and siblings for their love, patience and acceptance of my choosing the Red Road;

Ruthie Cromwell, my aunt, who has always offered a compassionate ear and enthusiastic support of the projects and adventures I've chosen;

Evan, a friend, confidante and great lover of Mother also.

The magical mountains of the Catoctins that call to me and have helped heal and inspire me.

My deepest gratitude with all of my heart.

CPSIA information can be obtained at www.ICGtesting.com
Printed in the USA
BVOW080646151012

302961BV00002B/2/P

9 780971 703230